SELECTED POEMS

WILLIAM BLA ... poets of the Roman ... ad to the poetry of ... o his contemporaries.

William Blake ... born in Broad Street in 1757, son of a London hosier. Apprenticed at an early age to an engraver, Blake was employed in 1779 by the bookseller J. Johnson. In 1782 he married Catherine Boucher, which was to be a lasting, though childless, union. He published his first volume, *Poetical Sketches*, in 1783 and set up a print shop a year after. He engraved and published *Songs of Innocence* in 1789, the same year as *The Book of Thel*, each of which covered the theme of a celebration of innocence. Blake's work became increasingly complex and visionary, and *The Marriage of Heaven and Hell* (engraved *c.* 1790-3), his principal prose work, is a sequence of paradoxes propounding his belief in the moral supremacy of imagination over reason. The raw energy of his writing is clearly revealed in his revolutionary works, *The French Revolution* (1791), *America: A Prophecy* (1793) and *Visions of the Daughters of Albion* (1793), while the visionary tone of Blake's poetic voice reached its peak in his *Songs of Experience* (1794); a series of short and accessible narrative poems, among them 'Tyger, Tyger' and 'Holy Thursday', injected with the pathos of lost innocence and strangled imagination, and a bitter insight into the power of oppression. The Blakes moved to Lambeth in 1790, where he continued to engrave his works and evolved his personal mythology in such writings as *The Book of Urizen* (1794), *Europe, A Prophecy* (1794), *The Song of Los* (1795) and the unfinished *Vala* (1797-1804). In 1803 Blake returned to London to work on his epics, *Milton* (1804-8) and *Jerusalem: The Emanation of the Giant Albion* (written and etched, 1804-20). In 1821 he was commissioned to produce illustrations for the Book of Job, published in 1826 and now greatly respected, and a later poem, *The Everlasting*

Gospel, reveals the undiminished power of his verse. However, during his lifetime Blake's poetry and art remained unappreciated by the public and was widely misinterpreted, and he was to spend the last years in relative obscurity leading up to his death in 1827.

Contained in this selection of Blake's poetry are *Poems from 'The Rosetti Manuscript'*, *The Pickering Manuscript*, and his immortal *Songs of Innocence and of Experience*, including 'The Chimney Sweeper', 'The Sick Rose' and 'London'.

PENGUIN POPULAR CLASSICS

SELECTED POEMS

WILLIAM BLAKE

PENGUIN BOOKS

PENGUIN BOOKS

Published by the Penguin Group
Penguin Books Ltd, 80 Strand, London WC2R ORL, England
Penguin Putnam Inc., 375 Hudson Street, New York, New York 10014, USA
Penguin Books Australia Ltd, Ringwood, Victoria, Australia
Penguin Books Canada Ltd, 10 Alcorn Avenue, Toronto, Ontario, Canada M4V 3B2
Penguin Books India (P) Ltd, 11 Community Centre, Panchsheel Park,
New Delhi – 110 017, India
Penguin Books (NZ) Ltd, Cnr Rosedale and Airborne Roads, Albany, Auckland,
New Zealand
Penguin Books (South Africa) (Pty) Ltd, 24 Sturdee Avenue, Rosebank 2196, South Africa

Penguin Books Ltd, Registered Offices: 80 Strand, London WC2R ORL, England

www.penguin.com

Blake's Poetical Works first published in Great Britain 1913
This selection published in Penguine Popular Classics 1996
6

Printed in England by Cox & Wyman Ltd, Reading, Berkshire

CONTENTS

iii

Contents

Contents

POEMS FROM 'THE ROSSETTI MANUSCRIPT'

I. EARLIER POEMS

v

Contents

Contents

vii

Contents

Contents

Contents

1789

Poetical

SKETCHES

BY W. B.

1783

I'm bereaved of my wife

MISCELLANEOUS POEMS

To Spring

O thou with dewy locks, who lookest down
Thro' the clear windows of the morning, turn
Thine angel eyes upon our western isle,
Which in full choir hails thy approach, O Spring!

The hills tell each other, and the list'ning   5
Valleys hear ; all our longing eyes are turnèd
Up to thy bright pavilions : issue forth,
And let thy holy feet visit our clime.

Come o'er the eastern hills, and let our winds
Kiss thy perfumèd garments ; let us taste   10
Thy morn and evening breath ; scatter thy pearls
Upon our love-sick land that mourns for thee.

O deck her forth with thy fair fingers ; pour
Thy soft kisses on her bosom ; and put
Thy golden crown upon her languish'd head,   15
Whose modest tresses were bound up for thee.

To Summer

O thou who passest thro' our valleys in
Thy strength, curb thy fierce steeds, allay the heat
That flames from their large nostrils ! thou, O Summer,
Oft pitched'st here thy golden tent, and oft
Beneath our oaks hast slept, while we beheld   5
With joy thy ruddy limbs and flourishing hair.

Beneath our thickest shades we oft have heard
Thy voice, when noon upon his fervid car
Rode o'er the deep of heaven; beside our springs
Sit down, and in our mossy valleys, on   10
Some bank beside a river clear, throw thy
Silk draperies off, and rush into the stream:
Our valleys love the Summer in his pride.

Our bards are fam'd who strike the silver wire:
Our youth are bolder than the southern swains: 15
Our maidens fairer in the sprightly dance:
We lack not songs, nor instruments of joy,
Nor echoes sweet, nor waters clear as heaven,
Nor laurel wreaths against the sultry heat.

To Autumn

O Autumn, laden with fruit, and stainèd
With the blood of the grape, pass not, but sit
Beneath my shady roof; there thou may'st rest,
And tune thy jolly voice to my fresh pipe,
And all the daughters of the year shall dance!   5
Sing now the lusty song of fruits and flowers.

'The narrow bud opens her beauties to
The sun, and love runs in her thrilling veins;
Blossoms hang round the brows of Morning, and
Flourish down the bright cheek of modest Eve,   10
Till clust'ring Summer breaks forth into singing,
And feather'd clouds strew flowers round her head.

'The spirits of the air live on the smells
Of fruit; and Joy, with pinions light, roves round
The gardens, or sits singing in the trees.'   15
Thus sang the jolly Autumn as he sat;
Then rose, girded himself, and o'er the bleak
Hills fled from our sight; but left his golden load.

To the Evening Star

To Winter

'O Winter ! bar thine adamantine doors :
The north is thine ; there hast thou built thy dark
Deep-founded habitation.   Shake not thy roofs,
Nor bend thy pillars with thine iron car.'

He hears me not, but o'er the yawning deep   5
Rides heavy ; his storms are unchain'd, sheathèd
In ribbèd steel ; I dare not lift mine eyes,
For he hath rear'd his sceptre o'er the world.

Lo ! now the direful monster, whose skin clings
To his strong bones, strides o'er the groaning rocks :   10
He withers all in silence, and in his hand
Unclothes the earth, and freezes up frail life.

He takes his seat upon the cliffs,—the mariner
Cries in vain.   Poor little wretch, that deal'st
With storms !—till heaven smiles, and the monster   15
Is driv'n yelling to his caves beneath mount Hecla.

To the Evening Star

Thou fair-hair'd angel of the evening,
Now, whilst the sun rests on the mountains, light
Thy bright torch of love ; thy radiant crown
Put on, and smile upon our evening bed !
Smile on our loves, and while thou drawest the   5
Blue curtains of the sky, scatter thy silver dew
On every flower that shuts its sweet eyes
In timely sleep.   Let thy west wind sleep on
The lake ; speak silence with thy glimmering eyes,
And wash the dusk with silver.   Soon, full soon,   10
Dost thou withdraw ; then the wolf rages wide,
And the lion glares thro' the dun forest :
The fleeces of our flocks are cover'd with
Thy sacred dew : protect them with thine influence.

Poetical Sketches

To Morning

O holy virgin ! clad in purest white,
Unlock heav'n's golden gates, and issue forth ;
Awake the dawn that sleeps in heaven ; let light
Rise from the chambers of the east, and bring
The honey'd dew that cometh on waking day.   5
O radiant morning, salute the sun
Rous'd like a huntsman to the chase, and with
Thy buskin'd feet appear upon our hills.

Fair Elenor

The bell struck one, and shook the silent tower ;
The graves give up their dead : fair Elenor
Walk'd by the castle gate, and lookèd in.
A hollow groan ran thro' the dreary vaults.

She shriek'd aloud, and sunk upon the steps,   5
On the cold stone her pale cheeks.   Sickly smells
Of death issue as from a sepulchre,
And all is silent but the sighing vaults.

Chill Death withdraws his hand, and she revives ;
Amaz'd, she finds herself upon her feet,   10
And, like a ghost, thro' narrow passages
Walking, feeling the cold walls with her hands.

Fancy returns, and now she thinks of bones
And grinning skulls, and corruptible death
Wrapp'd in his shroud ; and now fancies she hears   15
Deep sighs, and sees pale sickly ghosts gliding.

At length, no fancy but reality
Distracts her.   A rushing sound, and the feet
Of one that fled, approaches.——Ellen stood
Like a dumb statue, froze to stone with fear.   20

6

Fair Elenor

The wretch approaches, crying: 'The deed is done;
Take this, and send it by whom thou wilt send;
It is my life—send it to Elenor:—
He's dead, and howling after me for blood!

'Take this,' he cried; and thrust into her arms   25
A wet napkin, wrapp'd about; then rush'd
Past, howling: she receiv'd into her arms
Pale death, and follow'd on the wings of fear.

They pass'd swift thro' the outer gate; the wretch,
Howling, leap'd o'er the wall into the moat,   30
Stifling in mud.   Fair Ellen pass'd the bridge,
And heard a gloomy voice cry 'Is it done?'

As the deer wounded, Ellen flew over
The pathless plain; as the arrows that fly
By night, destruction flies, and strikes in darkness.   35
She fled from fear, till at her house arriv'd.

Her maids await her; on her bed she falls,
That bed of joy, where erst her lord hath press'd:
'Ah, woman's fear!' she cried; 'ah, cursèd duke!
Ah, my dear lord! ah, wretched Elenor!   40

'My lord was like a flower upon the brows
Of lusty May! Ah, life as frail as flower!
O ghastly death! withdraw thy cruel hand,
Seek'st thou that flow'r to deck thy horrid temples?

'My lord was like a star in highest heav'n   45
Drawn down to earth by spells and wickedness;
My lord was like the opening eyes of day
When western winds creep softly o'er the flowers;

'But he is darken'd; like the summer's noon
Clouded; fall'n like the stately tree, cut down;   50
The breath of heaven dwelt among his leaves.
O Elenor, weak woman, fill'd with woe!'

Thus having spoke, she raisèd up her head,
And saw the bloody napkin by her side,
Which in her arms she brought ; and now, tenfold   55
More terrifièd, saw it unfold itself.

Her eyes were fix'd ; the bloody cloth unfolds,
Disclosing to her sight the murder'd head
Of her dear lord, all ghastly pale, clotted
With gory blood ; it groan'd, and thus it spake :   60

'O Elenor, I am thy husband's head,
Who, sleeping on the stones of yonder tower,
Was 'reft of life by the accursèd duke !
A hirèd villain turn'd my sleep to death !

'O Elenor, beware the cursèd duke ;   65
O give not him thy hand, now I am dead ;
He seeks thy love ; who, coward, in the night,
Hirèd a villain to bereave my life.'

She sat with dead cold limbs, stiffen'd to stone ;
She took the gory head up in her arms ;   70
She kiss'd the pale lips ; she had no tears to shed ;
She hugg'd it to her breast, and groan'd her last.

Song

How sweet I roam'd from field to field
And tasted all the summer's pride,
Till I the Prince of Love beheld
Who in the sunny beams did glide !

He show'd me lilies for my hair,   5
And blushing roses for my brow ;
He led me through his gardens fair
Where all his golden pleasures grow.

How sweet, &c.] According to Malkin (*Father's Memoirs*, 1806 , this
poem was written by Blake before the age of fourteen.

With sweet May dews my wings were wet,
And Phoebus fir'd my vocal rage ;   10
He caught me in his silken net,
And shut me in his golden cage.

He loves to sit and hear me sing,
Then, laughing, sports and plays with me ;
Then stretches out my golden wing,   15
And mocks my loss of liberty.

Song

My silks and fine array,
My smiles and languish'd air,
By love are driv'n away ;
And mournful lean Despair
Brings me yew to deck my grave ;   5
Such end true lovers have.

His face is fair as heav'n
When springing buds unfold ;
O why to him was 't giv'n
Whose heart is wintry cold ?   10
His breast is love's all-worshipp'd tomb,
Where all love's pilgrims come.

Bring me an axe and spade,
Bring me a winding-sheet ;
When I my grave have made   15
Let winds and tempests beat :
Then down I'll lie as cold as clay.
True love doth pass away !

Song

Love and harmony combine,
And around our souls entwine
While thy branches mix with mine,
And our roots together join.

Joys upon our branches sit,   5
Chirping loud and singing sweet;
Like gentle streams beneath our feet
Innocence and virtue meet.

Thou the golden fruit dost bear,
I am clad in flowers fair;   10
Thy sweet boughs perfume the air,
And the turtle buildeth there.

There she sits and feeds her young'
Sweet I hear her mournful song;
And thy lovely leaves among,   15
There is love, I hear his tongue.

There his charming nest doth lay,
There he sleeps the night away;
There he sports along the day,
And doth among our branches play.   20

Song

I love the jocund dance,
The softly breathing song,
Where innocent eyes do glance,
And where lisps the maiden's tongue.

I love the laughing vale,   5
I love the echoing hill,
Where mirth does never fail,
And the jolly swain laughs his fill.

16 his] her; an obvious misprint, in the original.

Song

I love the pleasant cot,
I love the innocent bow'r,   10
Where white and brown is our lot.
Or fruit in the mid-day hour.

I love the oaken seat,
Beneath the oaken tree,
Where all the old villagers meet,   15
And laugh our sports to see.

I love our neighbours all,
But, Kitty, I better love thee;
And love them I ever shall;
But thou art all to me.   20

Song

Memory, hither come,
And tune your merry notes:
And, while upon the wind
Your music floats,
I'll pore upon the stream   5
Where sighing lovers dream,
And fish for fancies as they pass
Within the watery glass.

I'll drink of the clear stream,
And hear the linnet's song;   10
And there I'll lie and dream
The day along:
And when night comes, I'll go
To places fit for woe,
Walking along the darken'd valley   15
With silent Melancholy.

Mad Song

The wild winds weep,
And the night is a-cold;
Come hither, Sleep,
And my griefs unfold:
But lo! the morning peeps   5
Over the eastern steeps,
And the rustling beds of dawn
The earth do scorn.

Lo! to the vault
Of pavèd heaven,   10
With sorrow fraught
My notes are driven:
They strike the ear of night,
Make weep the eyes of day;
They make mad the roaring winds,   15
And with tempests play.

Like a fiend in a cloud,
With howling woe
After night I do crowd,
And with night will go;   20
I turn my back to the east
From whence comforts have increas'd;
For light doth seize my brain
With frantic pain.

17 Cp. 'Infant Sorrow' in the *Songs of Experience*:

> Helpless, naked, piping loud,
> Like a fiend hid in a cloud.

Song

Song

Fresh from the dewy hill, the merry year
Smiles on my head and mounts his flaming car;
Round my young brows the laurel wreathes a shade,
And rising glories beam around my head.

My feet are wing'd, while o'er the dewy lawn,　　　5
I meet my maiden risen like the morn:
O bless those holy feet, like angels' feet;
O bless those limbs, beaming with heav'nly light.

Like as an angel glitt'ring in the sky
In times of innocence and holy joy;　　　10
The joyful shepherd stops his grateful song
To hear the music of an angel's tongue.

So when she speaks, the voice of Heaven I hear;
So when we walk, nothing impure comes near;
Each field seems Eden, and each calm retreat;　　　15
Each village seems the haunt of holy feet.

But that sweet village where my black-eyed maid
Closes her eyes in sleep beneath night's shade,
Whene'er I enter, more than mortal fire
Burns in my soul, and does my song inspire.　　　20

Song

When early morn walks forth in sober grey,
Then to my black-eyed maid I haste away;
When evening sits beneath her dusky bow'r,
And gently sighs away the silent hour,
The village bell alarms, away I go,　　　5
And the vale darkens at my pensive woe.

To that sweet village, where my black-eyed maid
Doth drop a tear beneath the silent shade,
I turn my eyes; and pensive as I go
Curse my black stars and bless my pleasing woe.　　　10

13

Oft when the summer sleeps among the trees,
Whisp'ring faint murmurs to the scanty breeze,
I walk the village round ; if at her side
A youth doth walk in stolen joy and pride,
I curse my stars in bitter grief and woe,   15
That made my love so high and me so low.

O should she e'er prove false, his limbs I'd tear
And throw all pity on the burning air ;
I'd curse bright fortune for my mixèd lot,
And then I'd die in peace and be forgot.   20

To the Muses

Whether on Ida's shady brow,
Or in the chambers of the East,
The chambers of the sun, that now
From ancient melody have ceas'd ;

Whether in Heaven ye wander fair,   5
Or the green corners of the earth,
Or the blue regions of the air
Where the melodious winds have birth ;

Whether on crystal rocks ye rove,
Beneath the bosom of the sea   10
Wand'ring in many a coral grove,
Fair Nine, forsaking Poetry !

How have you left the ancient love
That bards of old enjoy'd in you !
The languid strings do scarcely move !   15
The sound is forc'd, the notes are few !

Gwin, King of Norway

Gwin King of Norway

Come, kings, and listen to my song:
When Gwin, the son of Nore,
Over the nations of the North
His cruel sceptre bore;

The nobles of the land did feed   5
Upon the hungry poor;
They tear the poor man's lamb, and drive
The needy from their door.

'The land is desolate; our wives
And children cry for bread;   10
Arise, and pull the tyrant down!
Let Gwin be humblèd!'

Gordred the giant rous'd himself
From sleeping in his cave;
He shook the hills, and in the clouds   15
The troubl'd banners wave.

Beneath them roll'd, like tempests black,
The num'rous sons of blood;
Like lions' whelps, roaring abroad,
Seeking their nightly food.   20

Down Bleron's hills they dreadful rush,
Their cry ascends the clouds;
The trampling horse and clanging arms
Like rushing mighty floods!

Their wives and children, weeping loud,   25
Follow in wild array,
Howling like ghosts, furious as wolves
In the bleak wintry day.

'Pull down the tyrant to the dust,
Let Gwin be humblèd,'
They cry, 'and let ten thousand lives   30
Pay for the tyrant's head.'

From tow'r to tow'r the watchmen cry,
'O Gwin, the son of Nore,
Arouse thyself! the nations, black   35
Like clouds, come rolling o'er!

Gwin rear'd his shield, his palace shakes,
His chiefs come rushing round;
Each, like an awful thunder cloud,
With voice of solemn sound: 40

Like rearèd stones around a grave
They stand around the King;
Then suddenly each seiz'd his spear,
And clashing steel does ring.

The husbandman does leave his plough   45
To wade thro' fields of gore;
The merchant binds his brows in steel,
And leaves the trading shore;

The shepherd leaves his mellow pipe,
And sounds the trumpet shrill;   50
The workman throws his hammer down
To heave the bloody bill.

Like the tall ghost of Barraton
Who sports in stormy sky,
Gwin leads his host, as black as night   55
When pestilence does fly,

With horses and with chariots—
And all his spearmen bold
March to the sound of mournful song,
Like clouds around him roll'd.   60

Gwin lifts his hand—the nations halt;
'Prepare for war!' he cries—
Gordred appears!—his frowning brow
Troubles our northern skies.

16

The armies stand, like balances   65
Held in th' Almighty's hand ;—
'Gwin, thou hast fill'd thy measure up:
Thou'rt swept from out the land.'

And now the raging armies rush'd
Like warring mighty seas ;   70
The heav'ns are shook with roaring war,
The dust ascends the skies !

Earth smokes with blood, and groans and shakes
To drink her children's gore,
A sea of blood ; nor can the eye   75
See to the trembling shore !

And on the verge of this wild sea
Famine and death doth cry ;
The cries of women and of babes
Over the field doth fly.   80

The King is seen raging afar,
With all his men of might ;
Like blazing comets scattering death
Thro' the red fev'rous night.

Beneath his arm like sheep they die,   85
And groan upon the plain ;
The battle faints, and bloody men
Fight upon hills of slain.

Now death is sick, and riven men
Labour and toil for life ;   90
Steed rolls on steed, and shield on shield,
Sunk in this sea of strife !

The god of war is drunk with blood ;
The earth doth faint and fail ;
The stench of blood makes sick the heav'ns ·   95
Ghosts glut the throat of hell !

O what have kings to answer for
Before that awful throne ;
When thousand deaths for vengeance cry,
And ghosts accusing groan !   100

Like blazing comets in the sky
That shake the stars of light,
Which drop like fruit unto the earth
Thro' the fierce burning night ;

Like these did Gwin and Gordred meet,   105
And the first blow decides ;
Down from the brow unto the breast
Gordred his head divides !

Gwin fell : the sons of Norway fled,
All that remain'd alive ;   110
The rest did fill the vale of death,
For them the eagles strive.

The river Dorman roll'd their blood
Into the northern sea ;
Who mourn'd his sons, and overwhelm'd   115
The pleasant south country.

An Imitation of Spenser

Golden Apollo, that thro' heaven wide
Scatter'st the rays of light, and truth's beams,
In lucent words my darkling verses dight,
And wash my earthy mind in thy clear streams,
That wisdom may descend in fairy dreams,   5
All while the jocund hours in thy train
Scatter their fancies at thy poet's feet ;
And when thou yields to night thy wide domain,
Let rays of truth enlight his sleeping brain.

For brutish Pan in vain might thee assay   10
With tinkling sounds to dash thy nervous verse,
Sound without sense; yet in his rude affray,
(For ignorance is Folly's leasing nurse
And love of Folly needs none other's curse)
Midas the praise hath gain'd of lengthen'd ears,   15
For which himself might deem him ne'er the worse
To sit in council with his modern peers,
And judge of tinkling rimes and elegances terse.

And thou, Mercurius, that with wingèd brow
Dost mount aloft into the yielding sky,   20
And thro' Heav'n's halls thy airy flight dost throw,
Entering with holy feet to where on high
Jove weighs the counsel of futurity;
Then, laden with eternal fate, dost go
Down, like a falling star, from autumn sky,   25
And o'er the surface of the silent deep dost fly:

If thou arrivest at the sandy shore
Where nought but envious hissing adders dwell,
Thy golden rod, thrown on the dusty floor,
Can charm to harmony with potent spell.   30
Such is sweet Eloquence, that does dispel
Envy and Hate that thirst for human gore;
And cause in sweet society to dwell
Vile savage minds that lurk in lonely cell.

O Mercury, assist my lab'ring sense   35
That round the circle of the world would fly,
As the wing'd eagle scorns the tow'ry fence
Of Alpine hills round his high aëry,
And searches thro' the corners of the sky,

15 ears] misprinted 'cares' in the original.

Sports in the clouds to hear the thunder's sound, 40
And see the wingèd lightnings as they fly;
Then, bosom'd in an amber cloud, around
Plumes his wide wings, and seeks Sol's palace high.

And thou, O warrior maid invincible,
Arm'd with the terrors of Almighty Jove, 45
Pallas, Minerva, maiden terrible,
Lov'st thou to walk the peaceful solemn grove,
In solemn gloom of branches interwove?
Or bear'st thy Ægis o'er the burning field,
Where, like the sea, the waves of battle move? 50
Or have thy soft piteous eyes beheld
The weary wanderer thro' the desert rove?
Or does th' afflicted man thy heav'nly bosom move?

Blind Man's Buff

When silver snow decks Susan's clothes,
And jewel hangs at th' shepherd's nose,
The blushing bank is all my care,
With hearth so red, and walls so fair;
'Heap the sea-coal, come, heap it higher, 5
The oaken log lay on the fire.'
The well-wash'd stools, a circling row,
With lad and lass, how fair the show!
The merry can of nut-brown ale,
The laughing jest, the love-sick tale, 10
Till, tir'd of chat, the game begins.
The lasses prick the lads with pins;
Roger from Dolly twitch'd the stool,
She, falling, kiss'd the ground, poor fool!

1, 2] Blake repeats these lines in the 'Song by an old Shepherd', with
change of 'Susan's' to 'Sylvia's', and 'th' shepherd's' (possibly a
printer's emendation) to 'shepherd's'.

Blind Man's Buff

She blush'd so red, with side-long glance 15
At hob-nail Dick, who griev'd the chance.
But now for Blind man's Buff they call;
Of each encumbrance clear the hall—
Jenny her silken 'kerchief folds,
And blear-eyed Will the black lot holds. 20
Now laughing stops, with 'Silence! hush!'
And Peggy Pout gives Sam a push.
The Blind man's arms, extended wide,
Sam slips between:—'O woe betide
Thee, clumsy Will!'—but titt'ring Kate 25
Is penn'd up in the corner straight!
And now Will's eyes beheld the play;
He thought his face was t'other way.
'Now, Kitty, now! what chance hast thou,
Roger so near thee!—Trips, I vow!' 30
She catches him—then Roger ties
His own head up—but not his eyes;
For thro' the slender cloth he sees,
And runs at Sam, who slips with ease
His clumsy hold; and, dodging round, 35
Sukey is tumbled on the ground!—
'See what it is to play unfair!
Where cheating is, there's mischief there.'
But Roger still pursues the chase,—
'He sees! he sees!' cries, softly, Grace; 40
'O Roger, thou, unskill'd in art,
Must, surer bound, go thro' thy part!
Now Kitty, pert, repeats the rimes,
And Roger turns him round three times,
Then pauses ere he starts—but Dick 45
Was mischief bent upon a trick;
Down on his hands and knees he lay
Directly in the Blind man's way,
Then cries out 'Hem!' Hodge heard, and ran
With hood-wink'd chance—sure of his man; 50

21

But down he came.—Alas, how frail
Our best of hopes, how soon they fail !
With crimson drops he stains the ground ;
Confusion startles all around.
Poor piteous Dick supports his head,   55
And fain would cure the hurt he made ;
But Kitty hasted with a key,
And down his back they straight convey
The cold relief ; the blood is stay'd,
And Hodge again holds up his head.   60
Such are the fortunes of the game,
And those who play should stop the same
By wholesome laws ; such as all those
Who on the blinded man impose
Stand in his stead ; as, long a-gone,   65
When men were first a nation grown,
Lawless they liv'd, till wantonness
And liberty began t' increase,
And one man lay in another's way ;
Then laws were made to keep fair play.   70

KING EDWARD THE THIRD

PERSONS.

King Edward.
The Black Prince.
Queen Philippa.
Duke of Clarence.
Sir John Chandos.
Sir Thomas Dagworth.
Sir Walter Manny.

Lord Audley.
Lord Percy.
Bishop.
William, Dagworth's
    Man.
Peter Blunt, a common
    Soldier.

SCENE.

The Coast of France.   King Edward and Nobles before it.
The Army.

King. O thou, to whose fury the nations are
But as dust, maintain thy servant's right !
Without thine aid, the twisted mail, and spear,
And forgèd helm, and shield of seven-times beaten brass,
Are idle trophies of the vanquisher.   5
When confusion rages, when the field is in a flame,
When the cries of blood tear horror from heav'n,
And yelling Death runs up and down the ranks,
Let Liberty, the charter'd right of Englishmen,
Won by our fathers in many a glorious field,   10
Enerve my soldiers ; let Liberty
Blaze in each countenance, and fire the battle.
The enemy fight in chains, invisible chains, but heavy ;
Their minds are fetter'd, then how can they be free ?
While, like the mounting flame,   15
We spring to battle o'er the floods of death !
And these fair youths, the flow'r of England,

Venturing their lives in my most righteous cause,
O sheathe their hearts with triple steel, that they
May emulate their fathers' virtues.   20
And thou, my son, be strong; thou fightest for a crown
That death can never ravish from thy brow,
A crown of glory—but from thy very dust
Shall beam a radiance, to fire the breasts
Of youth unborn! Our names are written equal   25
In fame's wide-trophied hall; 'tis ours to gild
The letters, and to make them shine with gold
That never tarnishes: whether Third Edward,
Or the Prince of Wales, or Montacute, or Mortimer,
Or ev'n the least by birth, shall gain the brightest fame,   30
Is in His hand to whom all men are equal.
The world of men are like the num'rous stars
That beam and twinkle in the depth of night,
Each clad in glory according to his sphere;
But we, that wander from our native seats   35
And beam forth lustre on a darkling world,
Grow larger as we advance: and some, perhaps
The most obscure at home, that scarce were seen
To twinkle in their sphere, may so advance
That the astonish'd world, with upturn'd eyes,   40
Regardless of the moon, and those that once were bright,
Stand only for to gaze upon their splendour.
     [*He here knights the Prince, and other young Nobles.*
Now let us take a just revenge for those
Brave Lords, who fell beneath the bloody axe
At Paris. Thanks, noble Harcourt, for 'twas   45
By your advice we landed here in Brittany,
A country not yet sown with destruction,
And where the fiery whirlwind of swift war
Has not yet swept its desolating wing.—
Into three parties we divide by day,   50
And separate march, but join again at night;
Each knows his rank, and Heav'n marshal all.   [*Exeunt.*

King Edward the Third

Clarence. My Lords, I have by the advice of her
Whom I am doubly bound to obey, my Parent
And my Sovereign, call'd you together.
My task is great, my burden heavier than
My unfledg'd years ;   5
Yet, with your kind assistance, Lords, I hope
England shall dwell in peace ; that, while my father
Toils in his wars, and turns his eyes on this
His native shore, and sees commerce fly round
With his white wings, and sees his golden London   10
And her silver Thames, throng'd with shining spires
And corded ships, her merchants buzzing round
Like summer bees, and all the golden cities
In his land overflowing with honey,
Glory may not be dimm'd with clouds of care.   15
Say, Lords, should not our thoughts be first to commerce ?
My Lord Bishop, you would recommend us agriculture ?
Bishop. Sweet Prince, the arts of peace are great,
And no less glorious than those of war,
Perhaps more glorious in the philosophic mind.   20
When I sit at my home, a private man,
My thoughts are on my gardens and my fields,
How to employ the hand that lacketh bread.
If Industry is in my diocese,
Religion will flourish ; each man's heart   25
Is cultivated and will bring forth fruit :
This is my private duty and my pleasure.
But, as I sit in council with my Prince,
My thoughts take in the gen'ral good of the whole,
And England is the land favour'd by Commerce ;   30
For Commerce, tho' the child of Agriculture,
Fosters his parent, who else must sweat and toil,
And gain but scanty fare. Then, my dear Lord,

Be England's trade our care ; and we, as tradesmen,
Looking to the gain of this our native land.   35
    Clar. O my good Lord, true wisdom drops like honey
From your tongue, as from a worshipp'd oak.
Forgive, my Lords, my talkative youth, that speaks
Not merely what my narrow observation has
Pick'd up, but what I have concluded from your lessons.   40
Now, by the Queen's advice, I ask your leave
To dine to-morrow with the Mayor of London :
If I obtain your leave, I have another boon
To ask, which is the favour of your company.
I fear Lord Percy will not give me leave.   45
    Percy. Dear Sir, a prince should always keep his state,
And grant his favours with a sparing hand,
Or they are never rightly valuèd.
These are my thoughts ; yet it were best to go
But keep a proper dignity, for now   50
You represent the sacred person of
Your father ; 'tis with princes as 'tis with the sun ;
If not sometimes o'er-clouded, we grow weary
Of his officious glory.
    Clar. Then you will give me leave to shine sometimes.   55
My Lord?
    Lord. Thou hast a gallant spirit, which I fear
Will be imposèd on by the closer sort.   [*Aside.*
    Clar. Well, I'll endeavour to take
Lord Percy's advice ; I have been usèd so much   60
To dignity that I'm sick on 't.
    Queen Phil. Fie, fie, Lord Clarence ! you proceed not to
      business,
But speak of your own pleasures.
I hope their Lordships will excuse your giddiness.
    Clar. My Lords, the French have fitted out many   65
Small ships of war, that, like to ravening wolves,
Infest our English seas, devouring all
Our burden'd vessels, spoiling our naval flocks.

The merchants do complain and beg our aid.

    Percy.   The merchants are rich enough ;   70
Can they not help themselves?

    Bish.   They can, and may ; but how to gain their will
Requires our countenance and help.

    Percy.   When that they find they must, my Lord, they will :
Let them but suffer awhile, and you shall see   75
They will bestir themselves.

    Bish.   Lord Percy cannot mean that we should suffer
This disgrace : if so, we are not sovereigns
Of the sea—our right, that Heaven gave
To England, when at the birth of nature   80
She was seated in the deep ; the Ocean ceas'd
His mighty roar, and fawning play'd around
Her snowy feet, and own'd his awful Queen.
Lord Percy, if the heart is sick, the head
Must be aggriev'd ; if but one member suffer,   85
The heart doth fail.   You say, my Lord, the merchants
Can, if they will, defend themselves against
These rovers : this is a noble scheme,
Worthy the brave Lord Percy, and as worthy
His generous aid to put it into practice.   90

    Percy.   Lord Bishop, what was rash in me is wise
In you ; I dare not own the plan.   'Tis not
Mine.   Yet will I, if you please,
Quickly to the Lord Mayor, and work him onward
To this most glorious voyage ; on which cast   95
I'll set my whole estate,
But we will bring these Gallic rovers under.

    Queen Phil.   Thanks, brave Lord Percy ; you have the thanks
Of England's Queen, and will, ere long, of England.   [*Exeunt*

SCENE. *At Cressy. Sir Thomas Dagworth and Lord Audley meeting.*

Audley   Good morrow, brave Sir Thomas ; the bright morn
Smiles on our army, and the gallant sun
Springs from the hills like a young hero
Into the battle, shaking his golden locks
Exultingly : this is a promising day.   5
  Dagworth   Why, my Lord Audley, I don't know.
Give me your hand, and now I'll tell you what
I think you do not know.   Edward's afraid of Philip.
  Audley.   Ha ! Ha ! Sir Thomas ! you but joke ;
Did you e'er see him fear ? At Blanchetaque,   10
When almost singly he drove six thousand
French from the ford, did he fear then ?
  Dagw.   Yes, fear—that made him fight so.
  Aud.   By the same reason I might say tis fear
That makes you fight.   15
  Dagw.   Mayhap you may : look upon Edward's face,
No one can say he fears ; but when he turns
His back, then I will say it to his face ;
He is afraid : he makes us all afraid.
I cannot bear the enemy at my back.   20
Now here we are at Cressy ; where to-morrow,
To-morrow we shall know.   I say, Lord Audley,
That Edward runs away from Philip.
  Aud.   Perhaps you think the Prince too is afraid ?
  Dagw.   No ; God forbid ! I'm sure he is not.   25
He is a young lion.   O ! I have seen him fight
And give command, and lightning has flashèd
From his eyes across the field :   I have seen him
Shake hands with death, and strike a bargain for
The enemy ; he has danc'd in the field   30
Of battle, like the youth at morris-play.
I'm sure he's not afraid, nor Warwick, nor none—

None of us but me, and I am very much afraid.

   Aud. Are you afraid too, Sir Thomas?
I believe that as much as I believe   35
The King's afraid: but what are you afraid of?

   Dagw. Of having my back laid open; we turn
Our backs to the fire, till we shall burn our skirts.

   Aud. And this, Sir Thomas, you call fear? Your fear
Is of a different kind then from the King's;   40
He fears to turn his face, and you to turn your back.
I do not think, Sir Thomas, you know what fear is.

Enter Sir John Chandos.

   Chand. Good morrow, Generals; I give you joy:
Welcome to the fields of Cressy. Here we stop,
And wait for Philip.   45

   Dagw. I hope so.

   Aud. There, Sir Thomas, do you call that fear?

   Dagw. I don't know; perhaps he takes it by fits.
Why, noble Chandos, look you here—
One rotten sheep spoils the whole flock;   50
And if the bell-wether is tainted, I wish
The Prince may not catch the distemper too.

   Chand. Distemper, Sir Thomas! what distemper?
I have not heard.

   Dagw. Why, Chandos, you are a wise man,   55
I know you understand me; a distemper
The King caught here in France of running away.

   Aud. Sir Thomas, you say you have caught it too.

   Dagw. And so will the whole army; 'tis very catching,
For, when the coward runs, the brave man totters.   60
Perhaps the air of the country is the cause.
I feel it coming upon me, so I strive against it;
You yet are whole; but, after a few more
Retreats, we all shall know how to retreat
Better than fight.—To be plain, I think retreating   65
Too often takes away a soldier's courage.

Chand.   Here comes the King himself : tell him your thoughts
Plainly, Sir Thomas.

Dagw.   I've told him before, but his disorder
Makes him deaf.   70

Enter King Edward and Black Prince.

King.   Good morrow, Generals ; when English courage fails,
Down goes our right to France.
But we are conquerors everywhere ; nothing
Can stand our soldiers ; each man is worthy
Of a triumph.   Such an army of heroes   75
Ne'er shouted to the Heav'ns, nor shook the field.
Edward, my son, thou art
Most happy, having such command : the man
Were base who were not fir'd to deeds
Above heroic, having such examples.   80

Prince.   Sire, with respect and deference I look
Upon such noble souls, and wish myself
Worthy the high command that Heaven and you
Have given me.   When I have seen the field glow,
And in each countenance the soul of war   85
Curb'd by the manliest reason, I have been wing'd
With certain victory ; and 'tis my boast,
And shall be still my glory, I was inspir'd
By these brave troops.

Dagw.   Your Grace had better make   90
Them all generals.

King.   Sir Thomas Dagworth, you must have your joke,
And shall, while you can fight as you did at
The Ford.

Dagw.   I have a small petition to your Majesty.   95

King   What can Sir Thomas Dagworth ask that Edward
Can refuse ?

Dagw.   I hope your Majesty cannot refuse so great
A trifle ; I've gilt your cause with my best blood,
And would again, were I not forbid   100

By him whom I am bound to obey: my hands
Are tièd up, my courage shrunk and wither'd,
My sinews slacken'd, and my voice scarce heard;
Therefore I beg I may return to England.

   King. I know not what you could have ask'd, Sir Thomas, 105
That I would not have sooner parted with
Than such a soldier as you have been, and such a friend:
Nay, I will know the most remote particulars
Of this your strange petition: that, if I can,
I still may keep you here.   110

   Dagw. Here on the fields of Cressy we are settled
Till Philip springs the tim'rous covey again.
The wolf is hunted down by causeless fear;
The lion flees, and fear usurps his heart,
Startled, astonish'd at the clam'rous cock;   115
The eagle, that doth gaze upon the sun,
Fears the small fire that plays about the fen.
If, at this moment of their idle fear,
The dog doth seize the wolf, the forester the lion,
The negro in the crevice of the rock   120
Doth seize the soaring eagle; undone by flight,
They tame submit: such the effect flight has
On noble souls.   Now hear its opposite:
The tim'rous stag starts from the thicket wild,
The fearful crane springs from the splashy fen,   125
The shining snake glides o'er the bending grass;
The stag turns head and bays the crying hounds,
The crane o'ertaken fighteth with the hawk,
The snake doth turn, and bite the padding foot.
And if your Majesty's afraid of Philip,   130
You are more like a lion than a crane:
Therefore I beg I may return to England.

   King. Sir Thomas, now I understand your mirth,
Which often plays with Wisdom for its pastime,
And brings good counsel from the breast of laughter.   135
I hope you'll stay, and see us fight this battle,

And reap rich harvest in the fields of Cressy;
Then go to England, tell them how we fight,
And set all hearts on fire to be with us.
Philip is plum'd, and thinks we flee from him,   140
Else he would never dare to attack us.   Now,
Now the quarry's set ! and Death doth sport
In the bright sunshine of this fatal day.

   Dagw.   Now my heart dances, and I am as light
As the young bridegroom going to be marrièd.   145
Now must I to my soldiers, get them ready,
Furbish our armours bright, new-plume our helms ;
And we will sing like the young housewives busièd
In the dairy : my feet are wing'd, but not
For flight, an please your grace.   150

   King.   If all my soldiers are as pleas'd as you,
'Twill be a gallant thing to fight or die ;
Then I can never be afraid of Philip.

   Dagw.   A raw-bon'd fellow t'other day pass'd by me ;
I told him to put off his hungry looks—   155
He answer'd me, 'I hunger for another battle.'
I saw a little Welshman with a fiery face ;
I told him he look'd like a candle half
Burn'd out ; he answer'd, he was 'pig enough
To light another pattle.'   Last night, beneath   160
The moon I walk'd abroad, when all had pitch'd
Their tents, and all were still ;
I heard a blooming youth singing a song
He had compos'd, and at each pause he wip'd
His dropping eyes.   The ditty was 'If he   165
Return'd victorious, he should wed a maiden
Fairer than snow, and rich as midsummer.'
Another wept, and wish'd health to his father.
I chid them both, but gave them noble hopes.
These are the minds that glory in the battle,   170
And leap and dance to hear the trumpet sound.

   King.   Sir Thomas Dagworth, be thou near our person :

Thy heart is richer than the vales of France:
I will not part with such a man as thee.
If Philip came arm'd in the ribs of death,   175
And shook his mortal dart against my head,
Thou'dst laugh his fury into nerveless shame!
Go now, for thou art suited to the work,
Throughout the camp; inflame the timorous,
Blow up the sluggish into ardour, and   180
Confirm the strong with strength, the weak inspire,
And wing their brows with hope and expectation:
Then to our tent return, and meet to council. [*Exit Dagworth.*

   Chand. That man's a hero in his closet, and more
A hero to the servants of his house   185
Than to the gaping world; he carries windows
In that enlargèd breast of his, that all
May see what's done within.

   Prince. He is a genuine Englishman, my Chandos,
And hath the spirit of Liberty within him.   190
Forgive my prejudice, Sir John; I think
My Englishmen the bravest people on
The face of the earth.

   Chand. Courage, my Lord, proceeds from self-dependence.
Teach man to think he's a free agent,   195
Give but a slave his liberty, he'll shake
Off sloth, and build himself a hut, and hedge
A spot of ground; this he'll defend; 'tis his
By right of Nature: thus set in action,
He will still move onward to plan conveniences,   200
Till glory fires his breast to enlarge his castle;
While the poor slave drudges all day, in hope
To rest at night.

   King. O Liberty, how glorious art thou!
I see thee hov'ring o'er my army, with   205
Thy wide-stretch'd plumes; I see thee
Lead them on to battle;
I see thee blow thy golden trumpet, while

Thy sons shout the strong shout of victory!
O noble Chandos, think thyself a gardener,   210
My son a vine, which I commit unto
Thy care: prune all extravagant shoots, and guide
Th' ambitious tendrils in the paths of wisdom;
Water him with thy advice; and Heav'n
Rain fresh'ning dew upon his branches! And,   215
O Edward, my dear son! learn to think lowly of
Thyself, as we may all each prefer other—
'Tis the best policy, and 'tis our duty.   [*Exit King Edward.*

   Prince. And may our duty, Chandos, be our pleasure.
Now we are alone, Sir John, I will unburden,   220
And breathe my hopes into the burning air,
Where thousand Deaths are posting up and down,
Commission'd to this fatal field of Cressy.
Methinks I see them arm my gallant soldiers,
And gird the sword upon each thigh, and fit   225
Each shining helm, and string each stubborn bow,
And dance to the neighing of our steeds.
Methinks the shout begins, the battle burns;
Methinks I see them perch on English crests,
And roar the wild flame of fierce war upon   230
The throngèd enemy! In truth I am too full
It is my sin to love the noise of war.
Chandos, thou seest my weakness; strong Nature
Will bend or break us: my blood, like a springtide,
Does rise so high to overflow all bounds   235
Of moderation; while Reason, in her
Frail bark, can see no shore or bound for vast
Ambition. Come, take the helm, my Chandos,
That my full-blown sails overset me not
In the wild tempest: condemn my venturous youth,   240
That plays with danger, as the innocent child
Unthinking plays upon the viper's den:
I am a coward in my reason, Chandos.
   Chand. You are a man, my Prince, and a brave man,

If I can judge of actions; but your heat 245
Is the effect of youth, and want of use:
Use makes the armèd field and noisy war
Pass over as a summer cloud, unregarded,
Or but expected as a thing of course.
Age is contemplative; each rolling year 250
Brings forth fruit to the mind's treasure-house:
While vacant youth doth crave and seek about
Within itself, and findeth discontent,
Then, tir'd of thought, impatient takes the wing,
Seizes the fruits of time, attacks experience, 255
Roams round vast Nature's forest, where no bounds
Are set, the swiftest may have room, the strongest
Find prey; till tired at length, sated and tired
With the changing sameness, old variety,
We sit us down, and view our former joys 260
With distaste and dislike.
   Prince.   Then, if we must tug for experience,
Let us not fear to beat round Nature's wilds,
And rouse the strongest prey: then, if we fall,
We fall with glory. I know the wolf 265
Is dangerous to fight, not good for food,
Nor is the hide a comely vestment; so
We have our battle for our pains. I know
That youth has need of age to point fit prey,
And oft the stander-by shall steal the fruit 270
Of th' other's labour. This is philosophy;
These are the tricks of the world; but the pure soul
Shall mount on native wings, disdaining
Little sport, and cut a path into the heaven of glory,
Leaving a track of light for men to wonder at. 275
I'm glad my father does not hear me talk;
You can find friendly excuses for me, Chandos.
But do you not think, Sir John, that if it please
Th' Almighty to stretch out my span of life,
I shall with pleasure view a glorious action 280

Which my youth master'd?

Chand. Considerate age, my Lord, views motives,
And not acts; when neither warbling voice
Nor trilling pipe is heard, nor pleasure sits
With trembling age, the voice of Conscience then,   285
Sweeter than music in a summer's eve,
Shall warble round the snowy head, and keep
Sweet symphony to feather'd angels, sitting
As guardians round your chair; then shall the pulse
Beat slow, and taste and touch and sight and sound and smell, 290
That sing and dance round Reason's fine-wrought throne,
Shall flee away, and leave them all forlorn;
Yet not forlorn if Conscience is his friend.   [*Exeunt.*

SCENE. *In Sir Thomas Dagworth's Tent. Dagworth, ana
William his Man.*

Dagw. Bring hither my armour, William.
Ambition is the growth of ev'ry clime.

Will. Does it grow in England, sir?

Dagw. Aye, it grows most in lands most cultivated.

Will. Then it grows most in France; the vines here are finer
than any we have in England.

Dagw. Aye, but the oaks are not.

Will. What is the tree you mentioned? I don't think I ever
saw it.

Dagw. Ambition.

Will. Is it a little creeping root that grows in ditches?

Dagw. Thou dost not understand me, William.
It is a root that grows in every breast;
Ambition is the desire or passion that one man
Has to get before another, in any pursuit after glory;
But I don't think you have any of it.

Will. Yes, I have; I have a great ambition to know every
thing, Sir.

Dagw. But when our first ideas are wrong, what follows must all be wrong, of course; 'tis best to know a little, and to know that little aright.

Will. Then, Sir, I should be glad to know if it was not ambition that brought over our King to France to fight for his right?

Dagw. Tho' the knowledge of that will not profit thee much, yet I will tell you that it was ambition.

Will. Then, if ambition is a sin, we are all guilty in coming with him, and in fighting for him.

Dagw. Now, William, thou dost thrust the question home; but I must tell you that, guilt being an act of the mind, none are guilty but those whose minds are prompted by that same ambition.

Will. Now, I always thought that a man might be guilty of doing wrong without knowing it was wrong.

Dagw. Thou art a natural philosopher, and knowest truth by instinct, while reason runs aground, as we have run our argument. Only remember, William, all have it in their power to know the motives of their own actions, and 'tis a sin to act without some reason.

Will. And whoever acts without reason may do a great deal of harm without knowing it.

Dagw. Thou art an endless moralist.

Will. Now there's a story come into my head, that I will tell your honour if you'll give me leave.

Dagw. No, William, save it till another time; this is no time for story-telling. But here comes one who is as entertaining as a good story!

Enter Peter Blunt.

Peter. Yonder's a musician going to play before the King; it's a new song about the French and English; and the Prince has made the minstrel a squire, and given him I don't know what, and I can't tell whether he don't mention us all one by one; and he is to write another about all us that are to die, that we may be remembered in Old England, for all our blood and bones are in France; and a great deal more that we shall all hear by and by:

and I came to tell your honour, because you love to hear war-songs.

Dagw. And who is this minstrel, Peter, dost know?

Peter. O aye, I forgot to tell that; he has got the same name as Sir John Chandos, that the Prince is always with—the wise man that knows us all as well as your honour, only ain't so good-natured.

Dagw. I thank you, Peter, for your information; but not for your compliment, which is not true. There's as much difference between him and me as between glittering sand and fruitful mould; or shining glass and a wrought diamond, set in rich gold, and fitted to the finger of an Emperor; such is that worthy Chandos.

Peter. I know your honour does not think anything of yourself, but everybody else does.

Dagw. Go, Peter, get you gone; flattery is delicious, even from the lips of a babbler. [*Exit Peter.*

Will. I never flatter your honour.

Dagw. I don't know that.

Will. Why, you know, Sir, when we were in England, at the tournament at Windsor, and the Earl of Warwick was tumbled over, you ask'd me if he did not look well when he fell; and I said no, he look'd very foolish; and you was very angry with me for not flattering you.

Dagw. You mean that I was angry with you for not flattering the Earl of Warwick. [*Exeunt.*

SCENE. *Sir Thomas Dagworth's Tent. Sir Thomas Dagworth—to him enter Sir Walter Manny.*

Sir Walter. Sir Thomas Dagworth, I have been weeping
Over the men that are to die to-day.

Dagw. Why, brave Sir Walter, you or I may fall.

Sir Walter. I know this breathing flesh must lie and rot,
Cover'd with silence and forgetfulness.—
Death wons in cities' smoke, and in still night,

6 wons] i.e. 'dwells', an archaism probably borrowed from Spenser.

When men sleep in their beds, walketh about!
How many in wallèd cities lie and groan,
Turning themselves upon their beds,
Talking with Death, answering his hard demands!　　10
How many walk in darkness, terrors are round
The curtains of their beds, destruction is
Ready at the door!　How many sleep
In earth, cover'd with stones and deathy dust,
Resting in quietness, whose spirits walk　　15
Upon the clouds of heaven, to die no more!
Yet death is terrible, tho' borne on angels' wings.
How terrible then is the field of Death,
Where he doth rend the vault of heaven,
And shake the gates of hell!　　20
O Dagworth, France is sick! the very sky,
Tho' sunshine light it, seems to me as pale
As the pale fainting man on his death-bed,
Whose face is shown by light of sickly taper
It makes me sad and sick at very heart,　　25
Thousands must fall to-day.

　　Dagw.　Thousands of souls must leave this prison-house,
To be exalted to those heavenly fields,
Where songs of triumph, palms of victory,
Where peace and joy and love and calm content　　30
Sit singing in the azure clouds, and strew
Flowers of heaven's growth over the banquet-table.
Bind ardent Hope upon your feet like shoes,
Put on the robe of preparation,
The table is prepar'd in shining heaven,　　35
The flowers of immortality are blown;
Let those that fight fight in good steadfastness,
And those that fall shall rise in victory.

　　Sir Walter.　I've often seen the burning field of war,
And often heard the dismal clang of arms;　　40
But never, till this fatal day of Cressy,
Has my soul fainted with these views of death.

I seem to be in one great charnel-house,
And seem to scent the rotten carcases ;
I seem to hear the dismal yells of Death,   45
While the black gore drops from his horrid jaws ;
Yet I not fear the monster in his pride—
But O ! the souls that are to die to-day !
   Dagw.   Stop, brave Sir Walter ; let me drop a tear,
Then let the clarion of war begin :   50
I'll fight and weep, 'tis in my country's cause ;
I'll weep and shout for glorious liberty.
Grim War shall laugh and shout, deckèd in tears,
And blood shall flow like streams across the meadows,
That murmur down their pebbly channels, and   55
Spend their sweet lives to do their country service :
Then shall England's verdure shoot, her fields shall smile,
Her ships shall sing across the foaming sea,
Her mariners shall use the flute and viol,
And rattling guns, and black and dreary war,   60
Shall be no more.
   Sir Walter.   Well, let the trumpet sound, and the drum beat ;
Let war stain the blue heavens with bloody banners ;
I'll draw my sword, nor ever sheathe it up
Till England blow the trump of victory,   65
Or I lay stretch'd upon the field of death.   [*Exeunt.*

SCENE.   *In the Camp.*   *Several of the Warriors meet at the King's*
    Tent with a Minstrel, who sings the following Song :

O sons of Trojan Brutus, cloth'd in war,
Whose voices are the thunder of the field,
Rolling dark clouds o'er France, muffling the sun
In sickly darkness like a dim eclipse,
Threatening as the red brow of storms, as fire   5
Burning up nations in your wrath and fury !

Your ancestors came from the fires of Troy,
(Like lions rous'd by light'ning from their dens,

Whose eyes do glare against the stormy fires),
Heated with war, fill'd with the blood of Greeks,   10
With helmets hewn, and shields coverèd with gore,
In navies black, broken with wind and tide:

They landed in firm array upon the rocks
Of Albion; they kiss'd the rocky shore;
'Be thou our mother and our nurse,' they said;   15
'Our children's mother, and thou shalt be our grave,
The sepulchre of ancient Troy, from whence
Shall rise cities, and thrones, and arms, and awful pow'rs.'

Our fathers swarm from the ships.   Giant voices
Are heard from the hills, the enormous sons   20
Of Ocean run from rocks and caves, wild men,
Naked and roaring like lions, hurling rocks,
And wielding knotty clubs, like oaks entangled
Thick as a forest, ready for the axe.

Our fathers move in firm array to battle;   25
The savage monsters rush like roaring fire,
Like as a forest roars with crackling flames,
When the red lightning, borne by furious storms,
Lights on some woody shore; the parchèd heavens
Rain fire into the molten raging sea.   30

The smoking trees are strewn upon the shore,
Spoil'd of their verdure.   O how oft have they
Defy'd the storm that howlèd o'er their heads!
Our fathers, sweating, lean on their spears, and view
The mighty dead: giant bodies streaming blood,   35
Dread visages frowning in silent death.

Then Brutus spoke, inspir'd; our fathers sit
Attentive on the melancholy shore:
Hear ye the voice of Brutus—'The flowing waves
Of time come rolling o'er my breast,' he said;   40
'And my heart labours with futurity:
Our sons shall rule the empire of the sea.

'Their mighty wings shall stretch from east to west.
Their nest is in the sea, but they shall roam
Like eagles for the prey; nor shall the young   45
Crave or be heard; for plenty shall bring forth,
Cities shall sing, and vales in rich array
Shall laugh, whose fruitful laps bend down with fulness.

'Our sons shall rise from thrones in joy,
Each one buckling on his armour; Morning   50
Shall be prevented by their swords gleaming,
And Evening hear their song of victory:
Their towers shall be built upon the rocks,
Their daughters shall sing, surrounded with shining spears.

'Liberty shall stand upon the cliffs of Albion,   55
Casting her blue eyes over the green ocean;
Or, tow'ring, stand upon the roaring waves,
Stretching her mighty spear o'er distant lands;
While, with her eagle wings, she covereth
Fair Albion's shore, and all her families.'   60

Prologue, intended for a Dramatic Piece of King Edward the Fourth

O for a voice like thunder, and a tongue
To drown the throat of war! When the senses
Are shaken, and the soul is driven to madness,
Who can stand? When the souls of the oppressèd
Fight in the troubled air that rages, who can stand?   5
When the whirlwind of fury comes from the
Throne of God, when the frowns of his countenance
Drive the nations together, who can stand?
When Sin claps his broad wings over the battle,
And sails rejoicing in the flood of Death;   10
When souls are torn to everlasting fire,
And fiends of Hell rejoice upon the slain,

Prologue to King John

O who can stand? O who hath caus̀ed thıs?
O who can answer at the throne of God?
The Kings and Nobles of the Land have done it!   15
Hear it not, Heaven, thy Ministers have done it!

Prologue to King John

Justice hath heaved a sword to plunge in Albion's breast; for Albion's sins are crimson dy'd, and the red scourge follows her desolate sons.   Then Patriot rose; full oft did Patriot rise, when Tyranny hath stain'd fair Albion's breast with her own children's gore.   Round his majestic feet deep thunders roll; each heart does tremble, and each knee grows slack.   The stars of heaven tremble; the roaring voice of war, the trumpet, calls to battle. Brother in brother's blood must bathe—rivers of death.   O land most hapless! O beauteous island, how forsaken! Weep from thy silver fountains, weep from thy gentle rivers! The angel of the island weeps.   Thy widowed virgins weep beneath thy shades. Thy aged fathers gird themselves for war.   The sucking infant lives to die in battle; the weeping mother feeds him for the slaughter.   The husbandman doth leave his bending harvest. Blood cries afar! The land doth sow itself! The glittering youth of courts must gleam in arms.   The aged senators their ancient swords assume.   The trembling sinews of old age must work the work of death against their progeny; for Tyranny hath stretch'd his purple arm, and 'Blood!' he cries; 'the chariots and the horses, the noise of shout, and dreadful thunder of the battle heard afar!' Beware, O proud! thou shalt be humbled; thy cruel brow, thine iron heart, is smitten, though lingering Fate is slow. O yet may Albion smile again, and stretch her peaceful arms, and raise her golden head exultingly! Her citizens shall throng about her gates, her mariners shall sing upon the sea, and myriads shall to her temples crowd! Her sons shall joy as in the morning! Her daughters sing as to the rising year!

A War Song to Englishmen

Prepare, prepare the iron helm of war,
Bring forth the lots, cast in the spacious orb;
Th' Angel of Fate turns them with mighty hands,
And casts them out upon the darken'd earth!
Prepare, prepare!   5

Prepare your hearts for Death's cold hand! prepare
Your souls for flight, your bodies for the earth;
Prepare your arms for glorious victory;
Prepare your eyes to meet a holy God!
Prepare, prepare!   10

Whose fatal scroll is that? Methinks 'tis mine!
Why sinks my heart, why faltereth my tongue?
Had I three lives, I'd die in such a cause,
And rise, with ghosts, over the well-fought field.
Prepare, prepare!   15

The arrows of Almighty God are drawn!
Angels of Death stand in the louring heavens!
Thousands of souls must seek the realms of light,
And walk together on the clouds of heaven!
Prepare, prepare!   20

Soldiers, prepare!   Our cause is Heaven's cause;
Soldiers, prepare!   Be worthy of our cause:
Prepare to meet our fathers in the sky:
Prepare, O troops, that are to fall to-day!
Prepare, prepare!   25

Alfred shall smile, and make his harp rejoice;
The Norman William, and the learnèd Clerk,
And Lion Heart, and black-brow'd Edward, with
His loyal queen, shall rise, and welcome us!
Prepare, prepare!   30

The Couch of Death

The Couch of Death

The veiled Evening walked solitary down the western hills, and Silence reposed in the valley; the birds of day were heard in their nests, rustling in brakes and thickets; and the owl and bat flew round the darkening trees: all is silent when Nature takes her repose.—In former times, on such an evening, when the cold clay breathed with life, and our ancestors, who now sleep in their graves, walked on the steadfast globe, the remains of a family of the tribes of Earth, a mother and a sister, were gathered to the sick bed of a youth. Sorrow linked them together; leaning on one another's necks alternately—like lilies dropping tears in each other's bosom— they stood by the bed like reeds bending over a lake, when the evening drops trickle down. His voice was low as the whisperings of the woods when the wind is asleep, and the visions of Heaven unfold their visitation. 'Parting is hard and death is terrible; I seem to walk through a deep valley, far from the light of day, alone and comfortless! The damps of death fall thick upon me! Horrors stare me in the face! I look behind, there is no returning; Death follows after me; I walk in regions of Death, where no tree is, without a lantern to direct my steps, without a staff to support me.' Thus he laments through the still evening, till the curtains of darkness were drawn. Like the sound of a broken pipe, the aged woman raised her voice. 'O my son, my son, I know but little of the path thou goest! But lo! there is a God, who made the world; stretch out thy hand to Him.' The youth replied, like a voice heard from a sepulchre, 'My hand is feeble, how should I stretch it out? My ways are sinful, how should I raise mine eyes? My voice hath used deceit, how should I call on Him who is Truth? My breath is loathsome, how should He not be offended? If I lay my face in the dust, the grave opens its mouth for me; if I lift up my head, sin covers me as a cloak. O my dear friends, pray ye for me! Stretch forth your hands that my Helper may come! Through the void space I walk, between the sinful world and eternity! Beneath me burns eternal fire! O for a hand to pluck me forth!' As the voice of an omen heard in the silent valley, when the few inhabitants cling trembling together; as the voice of the Angel of Death, when the thin beams of the moon give a faint light, such was this young man's voice to his friends. Like the bubbling waters of the brook in the dead of night, the aged woman raised her cry, and said, 'O Voice, that dwellest in my breast, can I not cry, and lift my eyes to Heaven? Thinking of this, my spirit is turned within me into confusion! O my child, my child, is thy breath infected? so is mine. As the deer wounded, by the brooks of water, so the arrows of sin stick in my flesh; the poison hath entered into my marrow.' Like rolling waves upon a desert shore, sighs succeeded sighs; they covered their faces and wept. The youth lay silent, his mother's arm was under his head; he was like a cloud tossed by the winds, till the sun shine, and the drops of rain glisten, the yellow harvest breathes, and the thankful eyes of the villagers are turned up in smiles. The traveller, that hath taken shelter under an oak, eyes the distant country with joy. Such smiles were seen upon the face of the youth: a visionary hand wiped away his tears, and a ray of light beamed around his head. All was still. The moon hung not out her lamp, and the stars faintly glimmered in the summer sky; the breath of night slept among the leaves of the forest; the bosom of the lofty hill drank in the silent dew, while on his majestic brow the voice of Angels is heard, and stringed sounds ride upon the wings of night. The sorrowful pair lift up their heads, hovering Angels are around them, voices of comfort are heard over the Couch of Death, and the youth breathes out his soul with joy into eternity.

Contemplation

Who is this, that with unerring step dares tempt the wilds, where only Nature's foot hath trod? 'Tis Contemplation, daughter of the grey Morning! Majestical she steppeth, and with her pure quill on every flower writeth Wisdom's name; now lowly bending, whispers in mine ear, 'O man, how great, how little, thou! O man, slave of each moment, lord of eternity! seest thou where Mirth sits on the painted cheek? doth it not seem ashamed of such a place, and grow immoderate to brave it out? O what an humble garb true Joy puts on! Those who want Happiness must stoop to find it; it is a flower that grows in every vale. Vain foolish man, that roams on lofty rocks, where, 'cause his garments are swoln with wind, he fancies he is grown into a giant! Lo, then, Humility, take it, and wear it in thine heart; lord of thyself, thou then art lord of all. Clamour brawls along the streets, and destruction hovers in the city's smoke; but on these plains, and in these silent woods, true joys descend: here build thy nest; here fix thy staff; delights blossom around; numberless beauties blow; the green grass springs in joy, and the nimble air kisses the leaves; the brook stretches its arms along the velvet meadow, its silver inhabitants sport and play; the youthful sun joys like a hunter roused to the chase, he rushes up the sky, and lays hold on the immortal coursers of day; the sky glitters with the jingling trappings. Like a triumph, season follows season, while the airy music fills the world with joyful sounds.' I answered, 'Heavenly goddess! I am wrapped in mortality, my flesh is a prison, my bones the bars of death; Misery builds over our cottage roofs, and Discontent runs like a brook. Even in childhood, Sorrow slept with me in my cradle; he followed me up and down in the house when I grew up; he was my schoolfellow: thus he was in my steps and in my play, till he became to me as my brother. I walked through dreary places with him, and in church-yards; and I oft found myself sitting by Sorrow on a tomb-stone.'

Samson

Samson, the strongest of the children of men, I sing; how he was foiled by woman's arts, by a false wife brought to the gates of death! O Truth! that shinest with propitious beams, turning our earthly night to heavenly day, from presence of the Almighty Father, thou visitest our darkling world with blessed feet, bringing good news of Sin and Death destroyed! O white-robed Angel, guide my timorous hand to write as on a lofty rock with iron pen the words of truth, that all who pass may read.—Now Night, noon-tide of damned spirits, over the silent earth spreads her pavilion, while in dark council sat Philista's lords; and, where strength failed, black thoughts in ambush lay. Their helmed youth and aged warriors in dust together lie, and Desolation spreads his wings over the land of Palestine: from side to side the land groans, her prowess lost, and seeks to hide her bruised head under the mists of night, breeding dark plots. For Dalila's fair arts have long been tried in vain; in vain she wept in many a treacherous tear. 'Go on, fair traitress; do thy guileful work; ere once again the changing moon her circuit hath performed, thou shalt overcome, and conquer him by force unconquerable, and wrest his secret from him. Call thine alluring arts and honest-seeming brow, the holy kiss of love, and the transparent tear; put on fair linen that with the lily vies, purple and silver; neglect thy hair, to seem more lovely in thy loose attire; put on thy country's pride, deceit, and eyes of love decked in mild sorrow; and sell thy lord for gold.' For now, upon her sumptuous couch reclined in gorgeous pride, she still entreats, and still she grasps his vigorous knees with her fair arms. 'Thou lov'st me not! thou 'rt war, thou art not love! O foolish Dalila! O weak woman! it is death clothed in flesh thou lovest, and thou hast been encircled in his arms! Alas, my lord, what am I calling thee? Thou art my God! To thee I pour my tears for sacrifice morning and evening. My days are covered with sorrow, shut up, darkened! By night I am deceived! Who says that thou wast born of mortal kind? Destruction was thy father, a lioness suckled thee, thy young hands tore human limbs, and gorged human flesh. Come hither, Death; art thou not Samson's servant? 'Tis Dalila that calls, thy master's wife; no, stay, and let thy master do the deed: one blow of that strong arm would ease my pain; then should I lay at quiet and have rest. Pity forsook thee at thy birth! O Dagon furious, and all ye gods of Palestine, withdraw your hand! I am but a weak

1 pen] misprinted 'pens'. Cp. 'Everlasting Gospel', γ l. 13.

woman.   Alas, I am wedded to your enemy!   I will go mad, and
tear my crisped hair; I'll run about, and pierce the ears o' th'
gods!   O Samson, hold me not; thou lovest me not!   Look not
upon me with those deathful eyes!   Thou wouldst my death,
and death approaches fast.'   Thus, in false tears, she bath'd his
feet, and thus she day by day oppressed his soul: he seemed
a mountain, his brow among the clouds; she seemed a silver
stream, his feet embracing.   Dark thoughts rolled to and fro in
his mind, like thunder clouds troubling the sky; his visage was
troubled; his soul was distressed.   'Though I should tell her all
my heart, what can I fear?   Though I should tell this secret of
my birth, the utmost may be warded off as well when told as now.'
She saw him moved, and thus resumes her wiles.   'Samson, I'm
thine; do with me what thou wilt: my friends are enemies; my
life is death; I am a traitor to my nation, and despised; my joy
is given into the hands of him who hates me, using deceit to the
wife of his bosom.   Thrice hast thou mocked me and grieved my
soul.   Didst thou not tell me with green withs to bind thy
nervous arms; and, after that, when I had found thy falsehood,
with new ropes to bind thee fast?   I knew thou didst but mock
me.   Alas, when in thy sleep I bound thee with them to try thy
truth, I cried, "The Philistines be upon thee, Samson!"   Then
did suspicion wake thee; how didst thou rend the feeble ties!
Thou fearest nought, what shouldst thou fear?   Thy power is
more than mortal, none can hurt thee; thy bones are brass, thy
sinews are iron.   Ten thousand spears are like the summer grass;
an army of mighty men are as flocks in the valleys; what canst
thou fear?   I drink my tears like water; I live upon sorrow!
O worse than wolves and tigers, what canst thou give when such
a trifle is denied me?   But O! at last thou mockest me, to shame
my over-fond inquiry.   Thou toldest me to weave thee to the
beam by thy strong hair; I did even that to try thy truth; but,
when I cried "The Philistines be upon thee!" then didst thou
leave me to bewail that Samson loved me not.'   He sat, and
inward griev'd; he saw and lov'd the beauteous suppliant, nor
could conceal aught that might appease her; then, leaning on her

bosom, thus he spoke: 'Hear, O Dalila! doubt no more of
Samson's love; for that fair breast was made the ivory palace of
my inmost heart, where it shall lie at rest: for sorrow is the lot
of all of woman born: for care was I brought forth, and labour is
my lot: nor matchless might, nor wisdom, nor every gift enjoyed,
can from the heart of man hide sorrow. Twice was my birth
foretold from heaven, and twice a sacred vow enjoined me that
I should drink no wine, nor eat of any unclean thing; for holy
unto Israel's God I am, a Nazarite even from my mother's womb.
Twice was it told, that it might not be broken. "Grant me
a son, kind Heaven," Manoa cried; but Heaven refused.
Childless he mourned, but thought his God knew best. In
solitude, though not obscure, in Israel he lived, till venerable age
came on: his flocks increased, and plenty crowned his board,
beloved, revered of man. But God hath other joys in store. Is
burdened Israel his grief? The son of his old age shall set it
free! The venerable sweetener of his life receives the promise first
from Heaven. She saw the maidens play, and blessed their
innocent mirth; she blessed each new-joined pair; but from her
the long-wished deliverer shall spring. Pensive, alone she sat
within the house, when busy day was fading, and calm evening,
time for contemplation, rose from the forsaken east, and drew the
curtains of heaven: pensive she sat, and thought on Israel's grief,
and silent prayed to Israel's God; when lo! an angel from the
fields of light entered the house. His form was manhood in the
prime, and from his spacious brow shot terrors through the
evening shade. But mild he hailed her, "Hail, highly favoured!"
said he; "for lo! thou shalt conceive, and bear a son, and Israel's
strength shall be upon his shoulders, and he shall be called
Israel's Deliverer. Now, therefore, drink no wine, and eat not
any unclean thing, for he shall be a Nazarite to God." Then, as
a neighbour, when his evening tale is told, departs, his blessing
leaving, so seemed he to depart: she wondered with exceeding
joy, nor knew he was an angel. Manoa left his fields to sit in the
house, and take his evening's rest from labour—the sweetest time
that God has allotted mortal man He sat, and heard with joy,

and praised God, who Israel still doth keep. The time rolled on, and Israel groaned oppressed. The sword was bright, while the ploughshare rusted, till hope grew feeble, and was ready to give place to doubting. Then prayed Manoa: "O Lord, thy flock is scattered on the hills! The wolf teareth them, Oppression stretches his rod over our land, our country is ploughed with swords, and reaped in blood. The echoes of slaughter reach from hill to hill. Instead of peaceful pipe the shepherd bears a sword, the ox-goad is turned into a spear. O when shall our Deliverer come? The Philistine riots on our flocks, our vintage is gathered by bands of enemies. Stretch forth thy hand, and save!" Thus prayed Manoa. The aged woman walked into the field, and lo! again the angel came, clad as a traveller fresh risen on his journey. She ran and called her husband, who came and talked with him. "O man of God," said he, "thou comest from far! Let us detain thee while I make ready a kid, that thou mayest sit and eat, and tell us of thy name and warfare; that, when thy sayings come to pass, we may honour thee." The Angel answered, "My name is Wonderful; inquire not after it, seeing it is a secret; but, if thou wilt, offer an offering unto the Lord."'

[END OF POETICAL SKETCHES]

APPENDIX TO POETICAL SKETCHES

Song by a Shepherd

> Welcome, stranger, to this place,
> Where joy doth sit on every bough,
> Paleness flies from every face ;
> We reap not what we do not sow.

> Innocence doth like a rose   5
> Bloom on every maiden's cheek ;
> Honour twines around her brows,
> The jewel health adorns her neck.

Song by an Old Shepherd

> When silver snow decks Sylvio's clothes,
> And jewel hangs at shepherd's nose,
> We can abide life's pelting storm,
> That makes our limbs quake, if our hearts be warm.

> Whilst Virtue is our walking-staff,   5
> And Truth a lantern to our path,
> We can abide life's pelting storm,
> That makes our limbs quake, if our hearts be warm.

> Blow, boisterous wind, stern winter frown,
> Innocence is a winter's gown.   10
> So clad, we'll abide life's pelting storm,
> That makes our limbs quake, if our hearts be warm.

These songs, which are written, though not in Blake's autograph, upon the fly-leaves of a presentation copy of the *Poetical Sketches*, dated May 15, 1784, were first printed by R. H. Shepherd in Pickering's reprint of 1868. Besides these, with the title 'Song 2ᵈ by a Young Shepherd', is an earlier version of the 'Laughing Song' in the *Songs of Innocence*.

SONGS

from

AN ISLAND IN THE MOON
(MS. *circa* 1784)

SONGS

FROM

AN ISLAND IN THE MOON

I

Little Phoebus came strutting in,
With his fat belly and his round chin.
What is it you would please to have?
Ho! Ho!
I won't let it go at only so and so!

II

Honour and Genius is all I ask,
And I ask the Gods no more!

No more! No more!
No more! No more! } *the three Philosophers bear chorus.*

The songs in this section are taken from the unfinished MS., without
title but known as *An Island in the Moon*, where they are sung by some of
the characters in that quaint satirical brochure. Among them, for the sake
of completeness, I include a few pieces of intentional doggerel, omitting only
three fragments which were not written by Blake, and the early versions of
three of the *Songs of Innocence*, the variant readings of which are given
elsewhere in the footnotes.

I and II] Sung by Quid the Cynic, MS.. chap. iii.

III

When Old Corruption first begun,
Adorn'd in yellow vest,
He committed on Flesh a whoredom—
O, what a wicked beast !

From then a callow babe did spring,   5
And Old Corruption smil'd
To think his race should never end,
For now he had a child.

He call'd him Surgery and fed
The babe with his own milk ;   10
For Flesh and he could ne'er agree :
She would not let him suck.

And this he always kept in mind ;
And form'd a crooked knife,
And ran about with bloody hands   15
To seek his mother's life.

And as he ran to seek his mother
He met with a dead woman.
He fell in love and married her—
A deed which is not common !   20

She soon grew pregnant, and brought forth
Scurvy and Spotted Fever,
The father grinn'd and skipt about,
And said 'I'm made for ever !

'For now I have procur'd these imps   25
I'll try experiments.'
With that he tied poor Scurvy down,
And stopt up all its vents.

III Sung by Quid the Cynic, MS., chap. vi.

And when the child began to swell
He shouted out aloud—
'I've found the dropsy out, and soon   30
Shall do the world more good.'

He took up Fever by the neck,
And cut out all its spots;
And, thro' the holes which he had made,   35
He first discover'd guts.

IV

Hear then the pride and knowledge of a sailor!
His sprit sail, fore sail, main sail, and his mizen.
A poor frail man—God wot! I know none frailer,
I know no greater sinner than John Taylor.

V

The Song of Phoebe and Jellicoe

Phoebe drest like beauty's queen,
Jellicoe in faint pea-green,
Sitting all beneath a grot,
Where the little lambkins trot.

Maidens dancing, loves a-sporting,   5
All the country folks a-courting,
Susan, Johnny, Bob, and Joe,
Lightly tripping on a row.

Happy people, who can be
In happiness compar'd with ye?   10
The pilgrim with his crook and hat
Sees your happiness complete.

IV Sung by Steelyard the Lawgiver, MS., chap. viii.
V Sung by Miss Gittipin, MS., chap. viii.

VI

Lo! the Bat with leathern wing,
Winking and blinking,
Winking and blinking,
Winking and blinking,
Like Dr. Johnson.

Quid. 'O ho!' said Dr. Johnson
To Scipio Africanus,

. . . .

. . . . . .

Suction. 'A ha!' to Dr. Johnson   10
Said Scipio Africanus,

. . . .

. . . .

And the Cellar goes down with a step. (*Grand Chorus.*)

VII

1st Vo.	Want Matches?
2nd Vo.	Yes! Yes! Yes!
1st Vo.	Want Matches?
2nd Vo.	No!
1st Vo.	Want Matches?
2nd Vo.	Yes! Yes! Yes!
1st Vo.	Want Matches?
2nd Vo.	No!

VI MS., chap. ix.
VII Song of boy match-sellers, MS., chap. ix.

VIII

As I walk'd forth one May morning
To see the fields so pleasant and so gay,
O! there did I spy a young maiden sweet,
Among the violets that smell so sweet,
                    smell so sweet,   5
                    smell so sweet,
Among the violets that smell so sweet.

IX

Hail Matrimony, made of Love!
To thy wide gates how great a drove
On purpose to be yok'd do come;
Widows and Maids and Youths also,
That lightly trip on beauty's toe,   5
Or sit on beauty's bum.

Hail fingerfooted lovely Creatures!
The females of our human natures,
Formèd to suckle all Mankind.
'Tis you that come in time of need,   10
Without you we should never breed,
Or any comfort find.

For if a Damsel's blind or lame,
Or Nature's hand has crook'd her frame,
Or if she's deaf, or is wall-eyed;   15
Yet, if her heart is well inclin'd,
Some tender lover she shall find
That panteth for a Bride.

VIII Sung by Steelyard the Lawgiver, MS., chap. ix.

IX Sung by Quid the Cynic, MS., chap. ix. The subject and metre of this song were perhaps suggested by 'He that intends to take a wife' (*Pills to purge Melancholy*, iii, p. 106).

The universal Poultice this,
To cure whatever is amiss   20
In Damsel or in Widow gay!
It makes them smile, it makes them skip;
Like birds, just curèd of the pip,
They chirp and hop away.

Then come, ye maidens! come, ye swains!   25
Come and be cur'd of all your pains
In Matrimony's Golden Cage—

X

To be or not to be
Of great capacity,
Like Sir Isaac Newton,
Or Locke, or Doctor South,
Or Sherlock upon Death—   5
I'd rather be Sutton!

For he did build a house
For agèd men and youth,
With walls of brick and stone;
He furnish'd it within   10
With whatever he could win,
And all his own.

He drew out of the Stocks
His money in a box,
And sent his servant   15
To Green the Bricklayer,
And to the Carpenter;
He was so fervent.

27 Here the song abruptly breaks off. With 'Matrimony's Golden Cage'
cp. the third stanza of 'How sweet I roam'd from field to field' in the
Poetical Sketches (p. 8).

X Sung by Obtuse Angle, MS., chap. ix.

6 Sutton] Thomas Sutton, founder of the Charterhouse (1532-1611).
Perhaps Obtuse Angle was an old Carthusian.

The chimneys were threescore,
The windows many more;   20
And, for convenience,
He sinks and gutters made,
And all the way he pav'd
To hinder pestilence.

Was not this a good man—   25
Whose life was but a span,
Whose name was Sutton—
As Locke, or Doctor South,
Or Sherlock upon Death,
Or Sir Isaac Newton?   30

XI

This city and this country has brought forth many mayors
To sit in state, and give forth laws out of their old oak chairs,
With face as brown as any nut with drinking of strong ale—
Good English hospitality, O then it did not fail!

With scarlet gowns and broad gold lace, would make a yeoman 5
    sweat;
With stockings roll'd above their knees and shoes as black as jet;
With eating beef and drinking beer, O they were stout and hale—
Good English hospitality, O then it did not fail!

Thus sitting at the table wide the mayor and aldermen
Were fit to give law to the city; each ate as much as ten: 10
The hungry poor enter'd the hall to eat good beef and ale—
Good English hospitality, O then it did not fail!

XI Sung by Steelyard the Lawgiver, MS., chap. ix. Cp. 'Old English
hospitality is long since deceased', in Chatterton's 'Antiquity of Christmas
Games', an essay reprinted in the *Miscellanies* of 1778, with which work
Blake appears to have been familiar.

XII

O, I say, you Joe,
Throw us the ball !
I've a good mind to go
And leave you all.
I never saw such a bowler   5
To bowl the ball in a tansy,
And to clean it with my hankercher
Without saying a word.

That Bill's a foolish fellow ;
He has given me a black eye.   10
He does not know how to handle a bat
Any more than a dog or a cat :
He has knock'd down the wicket,
And broke the stumps,
And runs without shoes to save his pumps.   15

XIII

Leave, O leave me to my sorrows ;
Here I'll sit and fade away,
Till I'm nothing but a spirit,
And I lose this form of clay.

Then if chance along this forest   5
Any walk in pathless ways,
Thro' the gloom he'll see my shadow
Hear my voice upon the breeze.

XII Sung by Tilly Lally, a schoolboy, MS., chap. xi.
XIII Sung by Miss Gittipin, MS., chap. xi.

XIV

There's Doctor Clash,
And Signor Falalasole,
O they sweep in the cash
Into their purse hole!
Fa me la sol, La me fa sol!   5

Great A, little A,
Bouncing B!
Play away, play away,
You're out of the key!
Fa me la sol, La me fa sol!   10

Musicians should have
A pair of very good ears,
And long fingers and thumbs,
And not like clumsy bears.
Fa me la sol, La me fa sol!   15

Gentlemen! Gentlemen!
Rap! Rap! Rap!
Fiddle! Fiddle! Fiddle!
Clap! Clap! Clap!
Fa me la sol, La me fa sol!   20

XIV Sung by Mr. Scropprell, MS., chap xi.

SONGS OF INNOCENCE
AND OF EXPERIENCE

(Engraved 1789–1794)

SONGS OF INNOCENCE

Introduction

Piping down the valleys wild,
Piping songs of pleasant glee,
On a cloud I saw a child,
And he laughing said to me:

'Pipe a song about a Lamb!'   5
So I piped with merry cheer.
'Piper, pipe that song again;'
So I piped: he wept to hear.

'Drop thy pipe, thy happy pipe;
Sing thy songs of happy cheer:'   10
So I sang the same again,
While he wept with joy to hear.

'Piper, sit thee down and write
In a book, that all may read.'
So he vanish'd from my sight,   15
And I pluck'd a hollow reed,

And I made a rural pen,
And I stain'd the water clear,
And I wrote my happy songs
Every child may joy to hear.   20

The Echoing Green

The Sun does arise,
And make happy the skies;
The merry bells ring
To welcome the Spring;
The skylark and thrush,   5
The birds of the bush,
Sing louder around
To the bells' cheerful sound,
While our sports shall be seen
On the Echoing Green.   10

Old John, with white hair,
Does laugh away care,
Sitting under the oak,
Among the old folk.
They laugh at our play,   15
And soon they all say:
'Such, such were the joys
When we all, girls and boys,
In our youth time were seen
On the Echoing Green.'   20

Till the little ones, weary,
No more can be merry;
The sun does descend,
And our sports have an end.
Round the laps of their mothers   25
Many sisters and brothers,
Like birds in their nest,
Are ready for rest,
And sport no more seen
On the darkening Green.   30

66

The Lamb

Little Lamb, who made thee?
Dost thou know who made thee?
Gave thee life, and bid thee feed,
By the stream and o'er the mead;
Gave thee clothing of delight,   5
Softest clothing, woolly, bright;
Gave thee such a tender voice,
Making all the vales rejoice?
   Little Lamb, who made thee?
   Dost thou know who made thee?   10

Little Lamb, I'll tell thee,
Little Lamb, I'll tell thee:
He is callèd by thy name,
For He calls Himself a Lamb.
He is meek, and He is mild;   15
He became a little child.
I a child, and thou a lamb,
We are callèd by His name.
   Little Lamb, God bless thee!
   Little Lamb, God bless thee!   20

The Shepherd

How sweet is the Shepherd's sweet lot!
From the morn to the evening he strays;
He shall follow his sheep all the day,
And his tongue shall be fillèd with praise.

For he hears the lamb's innocent call,   5
And he hears the ewe's tender reply;
He is watchful while they are in peace,
For they know when their Shepherd is nigh.

Songs of Innocence

Infant Joy

'I have no name :
I am but two days old.'
What shall I call thee ?
'I happy am,
Joy is my name.'   5
Sweet joy befall thee !

Pretty Joy !
Sweet Joy, but two days old.
Sweet Joy I call thee ·
Thou dost smile,   10
I sing the while,
Sweet joy befall thee !

The Little Black Boy

My mother bore me in the southern wild,
And I am black, but O ! my soul is white ;
White as an angel is the English child,
But I am black, as if bereav'd of light.

My mother taught me underneath a tree,   5
And, sitting down before the heat of day,
She took me on her lap and kiss'ed me,
And, pointing to the east, began to say :

'Look on the rising sun,—there God does live,
And gives His light, and·gives His heat away ;   10
And flowers and trees and beasts and men receive
Comfort in morning, joy in the noonday.

'And we are put on earth a little space,
That we may learn to bear the beams of love ;
And these black bodies and this sunburnt face   15
Is but a cloud, and like a shady grove.

The Little Black Boy

'For when our souls have learn'd the heat to bear,
The cloud will vanish; we shall hear His voice,
Saying: "Come out from the grove, My love and care,
And round My golden tent like lambs rejoice."'   20

Thus did my mother say, and kissèd me;
And thus I say to little English boy.
When I from black and he from white cloud free,
And round the tent of God like lambs we joy,

I'll shade him from the heat, till he can bear   25
To lean in joy upon our Father's knee;
And then I'll stand and stroke his silver hair,
And be like him, and he will then love me.

Laughing Song

When the green woods laugh with the voice of joy,
And the dimpling stream runs laughing by;
When the air does laugh with our merry wit,
And the green hill laughs with the noise of it;

When the meadows laugh with lively green,   5
And the grasshopper laughs in the merry scene,

Laughing Song] In an early MS. version of this song, written between
1783 and May 1784 (see Bibliographical Introduction), with the title 'Song
2^d by a Young Shepherd', the first two stanzas run as follows, the third
being identical with that of the engraved version:

> When the trees do laugh with our merry wit,
> And the green hill laughs with the noise of it;
> When the meadows laugh with lively green,
> And the grasshopper laughs in the merry scene;

> When the greenwood laughs with the voice of joy,
> And the dimpling stream runs laughing by,
> When Edessa and Lyca and Emilie
> With their sweet round mouths sing 'Ha, Ha, He!'

The name Lyca of stanza 2 reappears ten years later in 'The Little Girl
Lost' and 'The Little Girl Found' of the *Songs of Experience*.

When Mary and Susan and Emily
With their sweet round mouths sing 'Ha, Ha, He!'

When the painted birds laugh in the shade,
Where our table with cherries and nuts is spread,   10
Come live, and be merry, and join with me,
To sing the sweet chorus of 'Ha, Ha, He!'

Spring

      Sound the flute!
      Now it's mute.
      Birds delight
      Day and night;
      Nightingale   5
      In the dale,
      Lark in sky,
      Merrily,
Merrily, merrily, to welcome in the year.

      Little boy,   10
      Full of joy;
      Little girl,
      Sweet and small;
      Cock does crow,
      So do you;   15
      Merry voice,
      Infant noise,
Merrily, merrily, to welcome in the year.

      Little lamb,
      Here I am;   20
      Come and lick
      My white neck;
      Let me pull
      Your soft wool;
      Let me kiss   25
      Your soft face:
Merrily, merrily, we welcome in the year.

A Cradle Song

A Cradle Song

Sweet dreams, form a shade
O'er my lovely infant's head;
Sweet dreams of pleasant streams
By happy, silent, moony beams.

Sweet sleep, with soft down   5
Weave thy brows an infant crown.
Sweet sleep, Angel mild,
Hover o'er my happy child.

Sweet smiles, in the night
Hover over my delight;   10
Sweet smiles, mother's smiles,
All the livelong night beguiles.

Sweet moans, dovelike sighs,
Chase not slumber from thy eyes.
Sweet moans, sweeter smiles,   15
All the dovelike moans beguiles.

Sleep, sleep, happy child,
All creation slept and smil'd;
Sleep, sleep, happy sleep,
While o'er thee thy mother weep.   20

Sweet babe, in thy face
Holy image I can trace.
Sweet babe, once like thee,
Thy Maker lay and wept for me,

Wept for me, for thee, for all,   25
When He was an infant small.
Thou His image ever see,
Heavenly face that smiles on thee,

Smiles on thee, on me, on all;
Who became an infant small.   30
Infant smiles are His own smiles;
Heaven and earth to peace beguiles.

Songs of Innocence

Nurse's Song

When the voices of children are heard on the green,
And laughing is heard on the hill,
My heart is at rest within my breast,
And everything else is still.

'Then come home, my children, the sun is gone down,   5
And the dews of night arise;
Come, come, leave off play, and let us away
Till the morning appears in the skies.'

'No, no, let us play, for it is yet day,
And we cannot go to sleep;   10
Besides, in the sky the little birds fly,
And the hills are all cover'd with sheep.'

'Well, well, go and play till the light fades away,
And then go home to bed.'
The little ones leapèd and shoutèd and laugh'd   15
And all the hills echoèd.

Holy Thursday

'Twas on a Holy Thursday, their innocent faces clean,
The children walking two and two, in red and blue and green,
Grey-headed beadles walk'd before, with wands as white as snow,
Till into the high dome of Paul's they like Thames' waters flow.

Nurse's Song] An earlier version of this song is found in the MS. known
as *An Island in the Moon* (chap. xi), the first readings, most of which have
been there corrected to their present form, being noted below.   1 voices]
tongues *Isl. in Moon*.   2 And laughing upon the hill *Isl. in Moon 2nd
rdg*. (afterwards re-corrected to its earlier and present form).   5 Then come
home, children, the sun is down. *Isl. in Moon 1st rdg*.   10 And we
cannot sleep till it's dark *Isl. in Moon 1st rdg*.   11 The flocks are at play
and we can't go away *Isl. in Moon 1st rdg*.   12 And the meadows are
cover'd with sheep *Isl. in Moon 1st rdg*.

Holy Thursday] Engraved with some corrections from the original version,
which occurs in *An Island in the Moon* (chap. xi).   1 'Twas on a] Upon
a *Isl. in Moon*.   2 red] grey *Isl. in Moon*.

Holy Thursday

O what a multitude they seem'd, these flowers of London town! 5
Seated in companies they sit with radiance all their own.
The hum of multitudes was there, but multitudes of lambs,
Thousands of little boys and girls raising their innocent hands.

Now like a mighty wind they raise to Heaven the voice of song,
Or like harmonious thunderings the seats of Heaven among.   10
Beneath them sit the agèd men, wise guardians of the poor;
Then cherish pity, lest you drive an angel from your door.

The Blossom

Merry, merry sparrow!
Under leaves so green,
A happy blossom
Sees you, swift as arrow,
Seek your cradle narrow   5
Near my bosom.

Pretty, pretty robin!
Under leaves so green,
A happy blossom
Hears you sobbing, sobbing,   10
Pretty, pretty robin,
Near my bosom.

7 was] were *Isl. in Moon.*   8 And all in order sit waiting the chief
chanter's commands *Isl. in Moon 1st rdg. del.*; Thousands of little girls and
boys, etc. *ibid. 2nd rdg.*   9-12 In Blake's first draft this stood:

Then like a mighty wind they raise to heav'n the voice of song,
· Or like harmonious thunderings the seats of heav'n among,
When the whole multitude of innocents their voices raise
Like angels on the throne of heav'n, raising the voice of praise.

Blake then deleted the entire stanza, and began:

Let cherubim and seraphim now raise their voices high.

This also was cancelled, and the stanza rewritten with the slight changes
noted below.   9 Now] Then *Isl. in Moon.*   11 agèd] rev'rend *Isl. in
Moon.*   wise guardians] the guardians *Isl. in Moon.*

73

The Chimney Sweeper

When my mother died I was very young,
And my father sold me while yet my tongue
Could scarcely cry ''weep! 'weep! 'weep! 'weep!'
So your chimneys I sweep, and in soot I sleep.

There's little Tom Dacre, who cried when his head,   5
That curl'd like a lamb's back, was shav'd: so I said
'Hush, Tom! never mind it, for when your head's bare
You know that the soot cannot spoil your white hair.'

And so he was quiet, and that very night,
As Tom was a-sleeping, he had such a sight!—   10
That thousands of sweepers, Dick, Joe, Ned, and Jack,
Were all of them lock'd up in coffins of black.

And by came an Angel who had a bright key,
And he open'd the coffins and set them all free;
Then down a green plain leaping, laughing, they run,   15
And wash in a river, and shine in the sun.

Then naked and white, all their bags left behind,
They rise upon clouds and sport in the wind;
And the Angel told Tom, if he'd be a good boy,
He'd have God for his father, and never want joy.   20

And so Tom awoke; and we rose in the dark,
And got with our bags and our brushes to work.
Tho' the morning was cold, Tom was happy and warm;
So if all do their duty they need not fear harm.

The Divine Image

To Mercy, Pity, Peace, and Love
All pray in their distress;
And to these virtues of delight
Return their thankfulness.

For Mercy, Pity, Peace, and Love   5
Is God, our Father dear,
And Mercy, Pity, Peace, and Love
Is man, His child and care.

For Mercy has a human heart,
Pity a human face,   10
And Love, the human form divine,
And Peace, the human dress.

Then every man, of every clime,
That prays in his distress,
Prays to the human form divine,   15
Love, Mercy, Pity, Peace.

And all must love the human form,
In heathen, Turk, or Jew;
Where Mercy, Love, and Pity dwell
There God is dwelling too.   20

Night

The sun descending in the west,
The evening star does shine;
The birds are silent in their nest,
And I must seek for mine.
The moon, like a flower,
In heaven's high bower,   5
With silent delight
Sits and smiles on the night.

Farewell, green fields and happy groves,
Where flocks have took delight.   10
Where lambs have nibbled, silent moves
The feet of angels bright ;
Unseen they pour blessing,
And joy without ceasing,
On each bud and blossom,   15
And each sleeping bosom.

They look in every thoughtless nest,
Where birds are cover'd warm ;
They visit caves of every beast,
To keep them all from harm.   20
If they see any weeping
That should have been sleeping,
They pour sleep on their head,
And sit down by their bed.

When wolves and tigers howl for prey,   25
They pitying stand and weep ;
Seeking to drive their thirst away,
And keep them from the sheep.
But if they rush dreadful,
The angels, most heedful,   30
Receive each mild spirit,
New worlds to inherit.

And there the lion's ruddy eyes
Shall flow with tears of gold,
And pitying the tender cries,   35
And walking round the fold,
Saying 'Wrath, by His meekness,
And, by His health, sickness
Is driven away
From our immortal day.   40

Night

'And now beside thee, bleating lamb,
I can lie down and sleep;
Or think on Him who bore thy name,
Graze after thee and weep.
For, wash'd in life's river,   45
My bright mane for ever
Shall shine like the gold
As I guard o'er the fold.'

A Dream

Once a dream did weave a shade
O'er my Angel-guarded bed,
That an emmet lost its way
Where on grass methought I lay.

Troubled, 'wilder'd, and forlorn,   5
Dark, benighted, travel-worn,
Over many a tangled spray,
All heart-broke I heard her say:

'O, my children! do they cry?
Do they hear their father sigh?   10
Now they look abroad to see:
Now return and weep for me.'

Pitying, I dropp'd a tear;
But I saw a glow-worm near,
Who replied: 'What wailing wight   15
Calls the watchman of the night?

'I am set to light the ground,
While the beetle goes his round:
Follow now the beetle's hum;
Little wanderer, hie thee home.'   20

On Another's Sorrow

Can I see another's woe,
And not be in sorrow too?
Can I see another's grief,
And not seek for kind relief?

Can I see a falling tear,　　　　　　　5
And not feel my sorrow's share?
Can a father see his child
Weep, nor be with sorrow fill'd?

Can a mother sit and hear
An infant groan, an infant fear?　　　10
No, no! never can it be!
Never, never can it be!

And can He who smiles on all
Hear the wren with sorrows small,
Hear the small bird's grief and care,　15
Hear the woes that infants bear,

And not sit beside the nest,
Pouring pity in their breast;
And not sit the cradle near,
Weeping tear on infant's tear;　　　　20

And not sit both night and day,
Wiping all our tears away?
O, no! never can it be!
Never, never can it be!

He doth give His joy to all;　　　　　25
He becomes an infant small;
He becomes a man of woe;
He doth feel the sorrow too.

Think not thou canst sigh a sigh,
And thy Maker is not by;　　　　　　30
Think not thou canst weep a tear,
And thy Maker is not near.

O! He gives to us His joy
That our grief He may destroy;
Till our grief is fled and gone   35
He doth sit by us and moan.

The Little Boy Lost

'Father! father! where are you going?
O do not walk so fast.
Speak, father, speak to your little boy,
Or else I shall be lost.'

The night was dark, no father was there;   5
The child was wet with dew;
The mire was deep, and the child did weep,
And away the vapour flew.

The Little Boy Found

The little boy lost in the lonely fen,
Led by the wand'ring light,
Began to cry; but God, ever nigh,
Appear'd like his father, in white.

He kissèd the child, and by the hand led,   5
And to his mother brought,
Who in sorrow pale, thro' the lonely dale,
Her little boy weeping sought.

[END OF THE SONGS OF INNOCENCE]

The Little Boy Lost] From *An Island in the Moon* (chap. xi).   1 Father!
father!] O father, father *Isl. in Moon.*   3 Speak] O speak *Isl. in Moon.*
5 The night it was dark and no father was there *Isl. in Moon.*   6 The
child] And the child *Isl. in Moon.*

SONGS OF EXPERIENCE

Introduction

Hear the voice of the Bard!
Who present, past, and future, sees;
Whose ears have heard
The Holy Word
That walk'd among the ancient trees,   5

Calling the lapsèd soul,
And weeping in the evening dew;
That might control
The starry pole,
And fallen, fallen light renew!   10

'O Earth, O Earth, return!
Arise from out the dewy grass;
Night is worn,
And the morn
Rises from the slumberous mass.   15

'Turn away no more;
Why wilt thou turn away.
The starry floor,
The wat'ry shore,
Is giv'n thee till the break of day.'   20

Songs of Experience

Earth's Answer

> Earth rais'd up her head
> From the darkness dread and drear.
> Her light fled,
> Stony dread!
> And her locks cover'd with grey despair.　　　　5
>
> 'Prison'd on wat'ry shore,
> Starry Jealousy does keep my den:
> Cold and hoar,
> Weeping o'er,
> I hear the Father of the Ancient Men.　　　　10
>
> 'Selfish Father of Men!
> Cruel, jealous, selfish Fear!
> Can delight,
> Chain'd in night,
> The virgins of youth and morning bear?　　　　15

Earth's Answer] This and seventeen others of the *Songs of Experience* were engraved for this book from earlier drafts or transcripts in the *Rossetti MS.*, the original readings in each case being noted below.

Title] The Earth's Answer *MS. first word del.*　　　　3 Blake's successive changes of this line are :

> Her *eyes fled*
> *orbs dead*
> light fled (pencil).

10 Father of the] del. in MS., and replaced by some illegible word erased.
11-15 Cancelled in MS.　The original rime-arrangement abaab breaks down in this and the next stanza.　　　　11 Selfish] Cruel *MS. 1st rdg. del.*
12 selfish] weeping *MS. 1st rdg. del.*　　　　14 Chain'd] Clog'd *MS. 1st rdg. del.*

Earth's Answer

'Does spring hide its joy
When buds and blossoms grow?
Does the sower
Sow by night,
Or the ploughman in darkness plough?   20

'Break this heavy chain
That does freeze my bones around.
Selfish! vain!
Eternal bane!
That free Love with bondage bound.'   25

Nurse's Song

When the voices of children are heard on the green
And whisp'rings are in the dale,
The days of my youth rise fresh in my mind,
My face turns green and pale.

Then come home, my children, the sun is gone down,   5
And the dews of night arise;
Your spring and your day are wasted in play,
And your winter and night in disguise.

16-20 This stanza was an addition written in place of the third, which
Blake cancelled but restored when engraving.   16 joy] delight *MS. 1st
rdg. del.*   18. 19 Does the sower sow His seed by night *MS. 1st rdg. del.*
22 freeze] close *MS 1st rdg. del.*   24. 25 Thou, my bane Hast my Love
with bondage bound *MS 1st rdg. del.*
    Nurse's Song 3 The *dreams del. cha'gd to* 'da's'] of youth etc. *MS.*

The Fly

Little Fly,
Thy summer's play
My thoughtless hand
Has brush'd away.

Am not I   5
A fly like thee?
Or art not thou
A man like me?

For I dance,
And drink, and sing,   10
Till some blind hand
Shall brush my wing.

The Fly] In the first draft found in the *Rossetti MS.* Blake begins the song thus:

Woe! alas! my guilty hand
Brush'd across thy summer joy;
All thy gilded painted pride
Shatter'd, fled . . .

These unfinished lines were cancelled, and he then turned to the shorter metre, preserving the 'guilty hand' in the first draft of stanza i. Then follows a deleted stanza, omitted by him in the engraved version, probably because, since writing the poem, he had used its first two lines as one of his 'Proverbs of Hell' (*Marriage of Heaven and Hell*, p. 250):

The cut worm
Forgives the plough,
And dies in peace,
And so do thou.

Then come the second, third, and fifth stanzas in their present form, followed by two versions of stanza iv, which was an afterthought. Lastly, prefixed numbers were added, indicating the present order of the stanzas.

2 summer's] summer *MS.*   3 thoughtless] guilty *MS. 1st rdg. del.*

The Fly

If thought is life
And strength and breath,
And the want   15
Of thought is death;

Then am I
A happy fly,
If I live
Or if I die   20

The Tiger

Tiger! Tiger! burning bright
In the forests of the night,
What immortal hand or eye
Could frame thy fearful symmetry?

In what distant deeps or skies   5
Burnt the fire of thine eyes?
On what wings dare he aspire?
What the hand dare seize the fire?

And what shoulder, and what art,
Could twist the sinews of thy heart?   10
And when thy heart began to beat,
What dread hand? and what dread feet?

The Fly] 13-16   Thought is life
                       And strength and breath ·
                       But the want
                       Of thought is death.
MS. 1st rdg. del.

What the hammer? what the chain?
In what furnace was thy brain?
What the anvil? what dread grasp   15
Dare its deadly terrors clasp?

When the stars threw down their spears,
And water'd heaven with their tears,
Did he smile his work to see?
Did he who made the Lamb make thee?   20

Tiger! Tiger! burning bright
In the forests of the night,
What immortal hand or eye,
Dare frame thy fearful symmetry?

The original draft of 'The Tiger', written upon two opposite pages of the *Rossetti MS.*, enables us to follow every step in the composition of the poem. On the left-hand page is found the first rough cast of stanzas i, ii, iii, iv, and vi. In stanza iii the manuscript version throws light upon a verse which has proved a crux to many of Blake's readers and commentators. It will be seen from the appended transcript that Blake at first intended the line

    'What dread hand and what dread feet'

as the beginning of a sentence running on into the next quatrain. Dissatisfied with the form of this unfinished stanza, he cancelled it altogether, leaving the preceding line as it stood; but subsequently, when engraving the poem for the *Songs of Experience*, converted the passage, by a change of punctuation into its present shape:

    'What dread hand? & what dread feet?'

a line exactly parallel in form to

    'What the hammer? what the chain?'

of the following stanza. We have yet another reading in Dr. Malkin's *Father's Memoirs of his Child* (1806), where the version of 'The Tiger', presumably supplied to the author by Blake himself, contains the variant

    'What dread hand forged thy dread feet?'

On the opposite page of the *MS. Book* is the first draft of stanza v, and above it, though probably written after, a revised version of ii, which differs

The Tiger

from that finally adopted. To the right of these two stanzas follows a fair copy of i, iii, v, and vi, which, except for unimportant differences of capitalization, and the readings 'dare frame' for 'could frame' in the first, and 'hand and eye' for 'hand or eye' in the first and last stanzas, is identical with the text of the engraved *Songs*.

The following is a faithful transcript of the original draft of 'The Tiger' in the *MS*., Blake's variant readings being indicated typographically by placing them in consecutive order, one below another, deleted words or lines being printed in italics. The manuscript is unpunctuated throughout.

THE TYGER

1   Tyger Tyger burning bright
    In the forests of the night
    What immortal hand & eye
                        or
    Could frame thy fearful symmetry
    Dare

2   *In what* distant deeps or skies
    Burnt in
    Burnt the fire of thine eyes
    The cruel
    On what wings dare he aspire
    What the hand dare sieze the fire

3   And what shoulder & what art
    Could twist the sinews of thy heart
    And when thy heart began to beat
    What dread hand & what dread feet

    Could fetch it from the furnace deep
    And in thy horrid ribs dare steep
    In the well of sanguine woe
    In what clay & in what mould
    Were thy eyes of fury rolld

4   *What* the hammer   *what* the chain
    Where   *where*
    In what furnace was thy brain
    What the anvil   What *the arm*
                            arm
                            grasp
                            clasp
                        dread grasp

87

Could its deadly terrors *clasp*
Dare   *grasp*
                   clasp

6   Tyger Tyger burning bright
In the forests of the night
What immortal hand & eye
Dare *form* thy fearful symmetry
       frame

[*On the opposite page*]

Burnt in distant deeps or skies
The cruel fire of thine eyes
Could heart descend or wings aspire
What the hand dare sieze the fire

5   3   And *did he laugh* his work to see
       dare he *smile*
            laugh
     What the shoulder   what the knee
       ankle
   4   *Did* he who made the lamb make thee
      Dare
   1   When the stars threw down their spears
   2   And waterd heaven with their tears

The Little Girl Lost

In futurity
I prophetic see
That the earth from sleep
(Grave the sentence deep)

Shall arise and seek   5
For her Maker meek ;
And the desert wild
Become a garden mild.

The Little Girl Lost] This song and its sequel, 'The Little Girl Found,' were included in the early issues of the *Songs of Innocence*, but were transferred by Blake to the *Songs of Experience*, on the completion of the latter.

In the southern clime,
Where the summer's prime   10
Never fades away,
Lovely Lyca lay.

Seven summers old
Lovely Lyca told;
She had wander'd long   15
Hearing wild birds' song.

'Sweet sleep, come to me
Underneath this tree.
Do father, mother, weep?
Where can Lyca sleep?   20

'Lost in desert wild
Is your little child.
How can Lyca sleep
If her mother weep?

'If her heart does ache   25
Then let Lyca wake;
If my mother sleep,
Lyca shall not weep.

'Frowning, frowning night,
O'er this desert bright,   30
Let thy moon arise
While I close my eyes.'

Sleeping Lyca lay
While the beasts of prey,
Come from caverns deep,   35
View'd the maid asleep.

The kingly lion stood,
And the virgin view'd,
Then he gamboll'd round
O'er the hallow'd ground.   40

Leopards, tigers, play
Round her as she lay,
While the lion old
Bow'd his mane of gold

And her bosom lick,   45
And upon her neck
From his eyes of flame
Ruby tears there came ;

While the lioness
Loos'd her slender dress,   50
And naked they convey'd
To caves the sleeping maid.

The Little Girl Found

All the night in woe
Lyca's parents go
Over valleys deep,
While the deserts weep.

Tired and woe-begone,   5
Hoarse with making moan,
Arm in arm seven days
They trac'd the desert ways.

Seven nights they sleep
Among shadows deep,   10
And dream they see their child
Starv'd in desert wild.

Pale, thro' pathless ways
The fancied image strays
Famish'd, weeping, weak,   15
With hollow piteous shriek.

The Little Girl Found

Rising from unrest,
The trembling woman prest
With feet of weary woe:
She could no further go.   20

In his arms he bore
Her, arm'd with sorrow sore;
Till before their way
A couching lion lay.

Turning back was vain: 25
Soon his heavy mane
Bore them to the ground.
Then he stalk'd around,

Smelling to his prey;
But their fears allay   30
When he licks their hands,
And silent by them stands.

They look upon his eyes
Fill'd with deep surprise;
And wondering behold   35
A spirit arm'd in gold.

On his head a crown;
On his shoulders down
Flow'd his golden hair.
Gone was all their care.   40

'Follow me,' he said;
'Weep not for the maid;
In my palace deep
Lyca lies asleep.'

Then they followèd   45
Where the vision led,
And saw their sleeping child
Among tigers wild.

To this day they dwell
In a lonely dell;   50
Nor fear the wolfish howl
Nor the lions' growl.

The Clod and the Pebble

'Love seeketh not itself to please,
Nor for itself hath any care,
But for another gives its ease,
And builds a Heaven in Hell's despair.'

So sung a little Clod of Clay,   5
Trodden with the cattle's feet,
But a Pebble of the brook
Warbled out these metres meet:

'Love seeketh only Self to please,
To bind another to its delight,   10
Joys in another's loss of ease,
And builds a Hell in Heaven's despite.'

The Little Vagabond

Dear mother, dear mother, the Church is cold,
But the Ale-house is healthy and pleasant and warm;
Besides I can tell where I am used well,
Such usage in Heaven will never do well.

But if at the Church they would give us some ale,   5
And a pleasant fire our souls to regale,
We'd sing and we'd pray all the livelong day,
Nor ever once wish from the Church to stray.

The Clod and the Pebble] Title lacking in *MS*.   5 sung] sang *MS*.
The Little Vagabond] The little *pretty* Vagabond [*pretty* del.] *MS*.
4 Such usage in heaven makes all go to hell *MS. 1st rdg. del.*   The poor
parsons with wind like a blown bladder swell *MS. 2nd rdg.*

The Little Vagabond

Then the Parson might preach, and drink, and sing,
And we'd be as happy as birds in the spring;   10
And modest Dame Lurch, who is always at church,
Would not have bandy children, nor fasting, nor birch.

And God, like a father, rejoicing to see
His children as pleasant and happy as He,
Would have no more quarrel with the Devil or the barrel,   15
But kiss him, and give him both drink and apparel.

Holy Thursday

Is this a holy thing to see
In a rich and fruitful land,
Babes reduc'd to misery,
Fed with cold and usurous hand?

Is that trembling cry a song?   5
Can it be a song of joy?
And so many children poor?
It is a land of poverty!

And their sun does never shine,
And their fields are bleak and bare,   10
And their ways are fill'd with thorns:
It is eternal winter there.

For where'er the sun does shine,
And where'er the rain does fall,
Babe can never hunger there,   15
Nor poverty the mind appal.

---

13 rejoicing to see] that joys for to see *MS. 1st rdg. del.* 16 But shake
hands and kiss him and there'd be no more hell *MS. 1st rdg. del.* But kiss
him and give him both *food* [*del. changed to* 'drink'] and apparel *MS. 2nd rdg.*

Holy Thursday] 7 And so great a number poor *MS.*   8, 12 It is]
'Tis *MS.*   13 For] But *MS.*

A Poison Tree

I was angry with my friend :
I told my wrath, my wrath did end.
I was angry with my foe :
I told it not, my wrath did grow.

And I water'd it in fears,   5
Night and morning with my tears ;
And I sunnèd it with smiles,
And with soft deceitful wiles.

And it grew both day and night,
Till it bore an apple bright ;   10
And my foe beheld it shine,
And he knew that it was mine,

And into my garden stole
When the night had veil'd the pole :
In the morning glad I see   15
My foe outstretch'd beneath the tree.

The Angel

I dreamt a dream ! what can it mean ?
And that I was a maiden Queen,
Guarded by an Angel mild :
Witless woe was ne'er beguil'd !

And I wept both night and day,   5
And he wip'd my tears away,
And I wept both day and night,
And hid from him my heart's delight.

A Poison Tree] 'Christian Forbearance' *MS.* 4 A line drawn below this stanza in the MS. shows that Blake originally intended the poem to end at this point. 9 both] by *MS.* 11 And I gave it to my foe *MS.* 1st *rdg. del*

The Angel

So he took his wings and fled ;
Then the morn blush'd rosy red ;   10
I dried my tears, and arm'd my fears
With ten thousand shields and spears.

Soon my Angel came again :
I was arm'd, he came in vain ;
For the time of youth was fled,   15
And grey hairs were on my head.

The Sick Rose

O Rose, thou art sick !
The invisible worm,
That flies in the night,
In the howling storm,

Has found out thy bed   5
Of crimson joy ;
And his dark secret love
Does thy life destroy.

To Tirzah

Whate'er is born of mortal birth
Must be consumèd with the earth,
To rise from generation free :
Then what have I to do with thee?

The Angel] 15, 16 The same lines with a few slight verbal changes had
been used by Blake as the final couplets to two poems in the *Rossetti MS.*,
'Infant Sorrow' (p. 116), and 'In a Myrtle Snade (p. 119).   15 For]
But *MS. 1st rdg. del.*
The Sick Rose] 5 Hath found etc. *MS.*   7, 8 A dark secret love Doth
life destroy *MS. 1st rdg. del.*   7 his] her *MS.*
To Tirzah] This poem, of which there is no first draft in the *MS. Book*,
bears intrinsic evidence in its symbolism of having been composed at a much
later date than any of the other songs, the earliest issue in which it occurs
being a copy of the *Songs of Innocence and of Experience*, formerly in the
possession of Mr. Butts, and now in the Rowfant Library. Further proof of
this song being a late addition is found in Russell's *Engravings of William*

The sexes sprung from shame and pride,   5
Blow'd in the morn; in evening died;
But Mercy chang'd death into sleep;
The sexes rose to work and weep.

Thou, Mother of my mortal part,
With cruelty didst mould my heart,   10
And with false self-deceiving tears
Didst bind my nostrils, eyes, and ears;

Didst close my tongue in senseless clay,
And me to mortal life betray:
The death of Jesus set me free: 15
Then what have I to do with thee?

The Voice of the Ancient Bard

Youth of delight, come hither,
And see the opening morn,
Image of truth new-born.
Doubt is fled, and clouds of reason,
Dark disputes and artful teasing.   5
Folly is an endless maze,
Tangled roots perplex her ways.
How many have fallen there!
They stumble all night over bones of the dead,
And feel they know not what but care,   10
And wish to lead others, when they should be led.

Blake (no. 16, pp. 72-3), where he refers to a copy of the *Songs*, which, in place of 'To Tirzah', contains an engraving in colours representing a nude figure born aloft by winged cherubs. Perhaps, in spite of Blake's habit of repeating lines after a long interval of time, we may see some evidence of the approximate date of this poem in the fact that the final line of the first and last stanzas:

Then what have I to do with thee?

occurs also in the last poem of the *Pickering MS.* written *circa* 1801-3.

The Voice of the Ancient Bard] In all the early, as well as in most of the later issues, this was arranged as one of the *Songs of Innocence*.

My Pretty Rose-Tree

My Pretty Rose-Tree

>A flower was offer'd to me,
>Such a flower as May never bore ;
>But I said ' I've a pretty Rose-tree,'
>And I passèd the sweet flower o'er.
>
>Then I went to my pretty Rose-tree,   5
>To tend her by day and by night,
>But my Rose turn'd away with jealousy,
>And her thorns were my only delight.

Ah! Sun-Flower

>Ah, Sun-flower ! weary of time,
>Who countest the steps of the sun ;
>Seeking after that sweet golden clime,
>Where the traveller's journey is done ;
>
>Where the Youth pined away with desire,   5
>And the pale Virgin shrouded in snow,
>Arise from their graves, and aspire
>Where my Sun-flower wishes to go.

My Pretty Rose-Tree] Title wtg. in *MS.*   6 In the silence of the night *MS. 1st rdg. del.*   her] it *MS. 2nd rdg.*   7 turn'd away with jealousy] was turnèd from me *MS. 1st rdg. del. and replaced by* was fillèd with jealousy.   5–8 Blake's first version of this stanza may perhaps be preferred to that of the engraved *Songs* :

>Then I went to my pretty rose-tree
>In the silence of the night
>But my rose was turnèd from me,
>And her thorns were my only delight.

The Lily

    The modest Rose puts forth a thorn,
    The humble Sheep a threat'ning horn ;
    While the Lily white shall in love delight,
    Nor a thorn, nor a threat, stain her beauty bright.

The Garden of Love

    I went to the Garden of Love,
    And saw what I never had seen :
    A Chapel was built in the midst,
    Where I used to play on the green.

    And the gates of this Chapel were shut,   5
    And 'Thou shalt not' writ over the door ;
    So I turn'd to the Garden of Love
    That so many sweet flowers bore ;

The Lily] In its present form this little poem might more fitly rank as a Song of Innocence than as a Song of Experience ; but the first draft, with its successive alterations as seen in the *Rossetti MS.*, shows that Blake originally conceived it in its 'contrary state'. Beginning by writing :

    The rose puts envious . . .

he replaced this by 'The lustful rose', finishing the line with the words 'puts forth a thorn', and concluding thus :

    The coward sheep a threat'ning horn ;
    While the lily white shall in love delight,
    And the lion increase freedom and peace.

Returning to this piece, perhaps when about to engrave it as one of the *Songs*, Blake deleted the last line, substituting for it :

    The priest loves war, and the soldier peace—

but here, perceiving that his internal rime had disappeared, he cancelled this line also, and gave the poem an entirely different colour by changing the word 'lustful' to 'modest', and 'coward' to 'humble', and completing the quatrain (as in the engraved version) by a fourth line simply explanatory of the first three.

Title] Wtg. in *MS.*

The Garden of Love] Title wtg. in *MS.*   **2 And saw**] And I saw *MS.*   **7 So I**] And I *MS. 1st rdg. del.*

And I saw it was fillèd with graves,
And tomb-stones where flowers should be ;　　　10
And priests in black gowns were walking their rounds,
And binding with briars my joys and desires.

A Little Boy Lost

'Nought loves another as itself,
Nor venerates another so,
Nor is it possible to Thought
A greater than itself to know :

'And, Father, how can I love you　　　5
Or any of my brothers more?
I love you like the little bird
That picks up crumbs around the door.'

The Priest sat by and heard the child,
In trembling zeal he seiz'd his hair :　　　10
He led him by his little coat,
And all admir'd the priestly care.

And standing on the altar high,
Lo ! what a fiend is here,' said he,
'One who sets reason up for judge　　　15
Of our most holy Mystery.'

A Little Boy Lost] Then, Father, I cannot love you *MS. 1st rdg. del.*
6 Or] Nor *MS. 1st rdg. del.*　　　7 I love myself : so does the bird *MS. 1st rdg. del.*　　　11, 12 In the first draft :

The mother follow'd, weeping loud,
'O, that I such a fiend should bear !'

which was next changed to :

Then led him by his little coat
To shew his zealous priestly care.

The weeping child could not be heard,
The weeping parents wept in vain;
They stripp'd him to his little shirt,
And bound him in an iron chain;   20

And burn'd him in a holy place,
Where many had been burn'd before:
The weeping parents wept in vain.
Are such things done on Albion's shore?

Infant Sorrow

My mother groan'd, my father wept,
Into the dangerous world I leapt;
Helpless, naked, piping loud,
Like a fiend hid in a cloud.

Struggling in my father's hands,   5
Striving against my swaddling-bands,
Bound and weary, I thought best
To sulk upon my mother's breast.

The Schoolboy

I love to rise in a summer morn
When the birds sing on every tree;
The distant huntsman winds his horn,
And the skylark sings with me.
O! what sweet company.   5

19 They] And *MS. 1st. rdg. del.*
    19, 20 They bound the little ivory limbs
           In a cruel iron chain   *MS. 1st rdg. del.*
21 They burn'd him in a holy fire *MS. 1st rdg. del.*   24 Such things are
done on Albion's shore *MS. 1st rdg.*

Infant Sorrow] Cp. the much fuller form of this poem in the *Rossetti MS.*
(p. 115).

The Schoolboy] This song, like 'The Little Girl Lost', 'The Little Girl

The Schoolboy

But to go to school in a summer morn,
O! it drives all joy away;
Under a cruel eye outworn,
The little ones spend the day
In sighing and dismay.   10

Ah! then at times I drooping sit,
And spend many an anxious hour,
Nor in my book can I take delight,
Nor sit in learning's bower,
Worn thro' with the dreary shower.   15

How can the bird that is born for joy
Sit in a cage and sing?
How can a child, when fears annoy,
But droop his tender wing,
And forget his youthful spring?   20

O! father and mother, if buds are nipp'd
And blossoms blown away,
And if the tender plants are stripp'd
Of their joy in the springing day,
By sorrow and care's dismay,   25

How shall the summer arise in joy,
Or the summer fruits appear?
Or how shall we gather what griefs destroy,
Or bless the mellowing year,
When the blasts of winter appear?   30

Found', and 'The Voice of the Ancient Bard', originally formed one of the *Songs of Innocence*, and still appears as such in several of the later issues also.

London

I wander thro' each charter'd street,
Near where the charter'd Thames does flow,
And mark in every face I meet
Marks of weakness, marks of woe.

In every cry of every Man,   5
In every Infant's cry of fear,
In every voice, in every ban,
The mind-forg'd manacles I hear.

How the chimney-sweeper's cry
Every black'ning church appals;   10
And the hapless soldier s sigh
Runs in blood down palace walls.

But most thro' midnight streets I hear
How the youthful harlot's curse
Blasts the new-born infant's tear,   15
And blights with plagues the marriage hearse.

1, 2 charter'd] dirty *MS.*   3 And mark] And see *MS. 1st rdg. del.*
6 In every voice of every child *MS. 1st rdg. del.*   8 The german forged
links I hear *MS. 1st rdg. del.*

    9, 10 But most the chimney-sweeper's cry
        Blackens o'er the church's walls *MS. 1st rdg. del.*

13-16 In the MS. this stanza was at first written :

    But most the midnight harlot's curse
    From every dismal street I hear,
    Weaves around the marriage hearse,
    And blasts the new-born infant's tear.

This was cancelled and followed by :

    But most from every street I hear—

A Little Girl Lost

A Little Girl Lost

> *Children of the future age,*
> *Reading this indignant page,*
> *Know that in a former time,*
> *Love, sweet Love, was thought a crime!*

In the Age of Gold,   5
Free from winter's cold,
Youth and maiden bright
To the holy light,
Naked in the sunny beams delight.

Once a youthful pair,   10
Fill'd with softest care,
Met in garden bright
Where the holy light
Had just remov'd the curtains of the night.

There, in rising day,   15
On the grass they play ;
Parents were afar,
Strangers came not near,
And the maiden soon forgot her fear.

Tired with kisses sweet,   20
They agree to meet
When the silent sleep
Waves o'er heaven's deep,
And the weary tired wanderers weep.

alt. successively to
            . . . through wintry streets I hear
and   . . . the cry of youth I hear]
         How the midnight harlot's curse
         Blasts the new-born infant's tear,
         And *hangs* [*alt. to* smites] with plagues the marriage hearse.

To her father white 25
Came the maiden bright;
But his loving look,
Like the holy book,
All her tender limbs with terror shook.

'Ona! pale and weak! 30
To thy father speak:
O! the trembling fear.
O! the dismal care,
That shakes the blossoms of my hoary hair!'

The Chimney-sweeper

A little black thing among the snow,
Crying ''weep! 'weep!' in notes of woe!
'Where are thy father and mother, say?'—
'They are both gone up to the Church to pray

'Because I was happy upon the heath, 5
And smil'd among the winter's snow,
They clothèd me in the clothes of death,
And taught me to sing the notes of woe.

'And because I am happy and dance and sing,
They think they have done me no injury, 10
And are gone to praise God and His Priest and King,
Who make up a Heaven of our misery.'

The Chimney-sweeper] The original draft of this song in the *Rossetti MS.*
shows that Blake at first intended the second and third stanzas to form a poem
complete in itself. The first stanza and title were an afterthought, written
in pencil upon a different page. Cp. also the quatrain placed by me among
Gnomic Verses (p. 194), 'There souls of men are bought and sold,' which
may possibly have been written with the intention of its forming another
stanza of this song.   3 Where are they, father and mother, say? *MS.*
4 to the church] to church *MS.*   6 winter's snow] wintry *wind*
[*alt. to* snow] *MS.*   12 Who wrap themselves up in our misery *MS.*
1st rdg. del.

The Human Abstract

The Human Abstract

Pity would be no more
If we did not make somebody poor;
And Mercy no more could be
If all were as happy as we.

And mutual fear brings peace,   5
Till the selfish loves increase:
Then Cruelty knits a snare,
And spreads his baits with care.

He sits down with holy fears,
And waters the ground with tears;   10
Then Humility takes its root
Underneath his foot.

Soon spreads the dismal shade
Of Mystery over his head;
And the caterpillar and fly   15
Feed on the Mystery.

And it bears the fruit of Deceit,
Ruddy and sweet to eat;
And the raven his nest has made
In its thickest shade.   20

Title] 'The Earth' *1st rdg.* cancelled, and changed to 'The Human Image'.   1 would] could *MS.*   2 If there was nobody poor *MS. 1st rdg. del.*   20 thickest] blackest *MS.*

The Gods of the earth and sea
Sought thro' Nature to find this tree;
But their search was all in vain:
There grows one in the Human brain.

[END OF THE SONGS OF EXPERIENCE]

APPENDIX

TO THE SONGS OF INNOCENCE AND OF EXPERIENCE

A Divine Image

Cruelty has a human heart,
And Jealousy a human face;
Terror the human form divine,
And Secrecy the human dress.

The human dress is forgèd iron,   5
The human form a fiery forge,
The human face a furnace seal'd,
The human heart its hungry gorge.

23, 24 But their search was all in vain
Till they sought in the human brain.

MS. 1st rdg., last line del.

A Divine Image] This song cannot, strictly speaking, be regarded as part
of the foregoing book. A companion poem to 'The Divine Image' (p. 75),
it seems to have been engraved by Blake in the same manner as the rest,
with a view to its forming one of the *Songs of Experience*. It was not, how-
ever, included in any authentic copy of the *Songs* issued during the author's
lifetime, and is only found in an uncoloured impression in the British
Museum Reading Room copy, where the watermark of the paper, which is
dated 1832, proves that it must have been printed, perhaps by Tatham, at
least five years after Blake's death.

P O E M S

from

'THE ROSSETTI MANUSCRIPT'

(*circa* 1793–1811)

sometimes called

'THE MANUSCRIPT BOOK'

POEMS FROM THE ROSSETTI MS.

I

Written *circa* 1793

Never seek to tell thy Love

Never seek to tell thy love,
Love that never told can be;
For the gentle wind does move
Silently, invisibly.

I told my love, I told my love,   5
I told her all my heart;
Trembling, cold, in ghastly fears,
Ah! she doth depart.

Soon as she was gone from me,
A traveller came by,   10
Silently, invisibly:
He took her with a sigh.

In this section are included all the poems in the *Rossetti MS.*, arranged in the order in which they occur, with the exception of the early versions of some of the *Songs of Experience* (the variant readings of which are given in footnotes), and the gnomic verses, epigrams, and short satirical pieces which I group together elsewhere.

Never seek, &c.] I give here the earlier and incomparably finer version of this song, which Blake subsequently altered by cancelling the first stanza (after changing 'seek' to 'pain' in l. 1), and substituting

'O! was no deny'

for the concluding line of the poem.

I laid me down upon a Bank

I laid me down upon a bank,
Where Love lay sleeping;
I heard among the rushes dank
Weeping, weeping.

Then I went to the heath and the wild,   5
To the thistles and thorns of the waste;
And they told me how they were beguil'd,
Driven out, and compell'd to be chaste.

I saw a Chapel all of Gold

I saw a Chapel all of gold
That none did dare to enter in,
And many weeping stood without,
Weeping, mourning, worshipping.

I saw a Serpent rise between   5
The white pillars of the door,
And he forc'd and forc'd and forc'd;
Down the golden hinges tore,

And along the pavement sweet,
Set with pearls and rubies bright,   10
All his shining length he drew,
Till upon the altar white

Vomiting his poison out
On the Bread and on the Wine.
So I turn'd into a sty,   15
And laid me down among the swine.

I saw a Chapel, &c.] 8 Till he broke the pearly door *MS. 1st rdg. del.*

I asked a Thief

I asked a Thief

I askèd a thief to steal me a peach :
He turnèd up his eyes.
I ask'd a lithe lady to lie her down :
Holy and meek, she cries.

As soon as I went   5
An Angel came :
He wink'd at the thief,
And smil'd at the dame ;

And without one word said
Had a peach from the tree,   10
And still as a maid
Enjoy'd the lady.

I heard an Angel singing

I heard an Angel singing
When the day was springing :
'Mercy, Pity, Peace
Is the world's release.'

Thus he sang all day   5
Over the new-mown hay,
Till the sun went down,
And haycocks lookèd brown.

I asked a Thief] 2 And he turnèd etc. *MS. 1st rdg. del.*   5, 6 Blake
writes as a single line.   7 He] And he *MS. 1st rdg. del.*   9 said]
spoke *MS. 1st rdg. del.*   11 And 'twixt earnest and joke *MS. 1st rdg. del.*
12 Enjoy'd] He enjoy'd *MS. 1st rdg. del.*

I heard an Angel singing] A variant version of 'The Human Image',
engraved under the title 'The Human Abstract' in the *Songs of Experience*

I heard a Devil curse
Over the heath and the furze :   10
'Mercy could be no more
If there was nobody poor,

'And Pity no more could be,
If all were as happy as we.'
At his curse the sun went down,   15
And the heavens gave a frown.

[Down pour'd the heavy rain
Over the new reap'd grain ;
And Misery's increase
Is Mercy, Pity, Peace.]   20

---

15 At his curse] Thus he sang and *MS. 1st rdg. del.*   16 Here, as the
MS. indicates, the poem originally ended, Blake afterwards adding a fifth
stanza :

> Down [at first *And down*] pour'd the heavy rain
> Over the new-reap'd grain,
> And Mercy and Pity and Peace descended ;
> The Farmers were ruined and harvest was ended—

and again marking the completion of the piece by a fresh terminal line.
This entire stanza was afterwards deleted, and is followed by several attempts
at a new couplet, rehandling in the original metre the theme of Mercy, Pity,
Peace, all of which were cancelled with the exception of the final reading :

> And Misery's increase
> Is Mercy, Pity, Peace.

These lines seem intended to form the final couplet of v, and Swinburne
doubtless interprets rightly the author's intention in appending them to the
first deleted couplet :

> Down pour'd the heavy rain
> Over the new-reap'd grain,

and printing this additional stanza in the form in which it appears, in square
brackets, in my text.

A Cradle Song

A Cradle Song

Sleep! sleep! beauty bright,
Dreaming o'er the joys of night;
Sleep! sleep! in thy sleep
Little sorrows sit and weep.

Sweet Babe, in thy face   5
Soft desires I can trace,
Secret joys and secret smiles,
Little pretty infant wiles.

As thy softest limbs I feel,
Smiles as of the morning steal   10
O'er thy cheek, and o'er thy breast
Where thy little heart does rest.

O! the cunning wiles that creep
In thy little heart asleep.
When thy little heart does wake   15
Then the dreadful lightnings break,

From thy cheek and from thy eye,
O'er the youthful harvests nigh.
Infant wiles and infant smiles
Heaven and Earth of peace beguiles.   20

A Cradle Song] Obviously designed as the contrary of 'A Cradle Song' in the *Songs of Innocence*. As first written the poem consisted of stanzas i, iii, and iv; stanza ii was then added and the end of the song indicated by a new terminal line, while still later Blake appended a final stanza and numbered the whole in their present order.

1–4 The two couplets were originally written in reverse order. 2 Thou shalt taste the joys of night *MS. 1st rdg. del.* 4 Thou wilt every secret keep *MS. 1st rdg. del.* Canst thou any secret keep *MS. 2nd rdg. del.* 8 Such as burning youth beguiles *MS. 1st rdg. del.*

9, 10 Yet a little while the moon
                    Silent—   *abandoned opening of this stanza.*
9 feel] touch *MS. 1st rdg. del.*; stroke *MS. 2nd rdg. del.* 10 steal] broke *MS. 1st rdg. del.* 19 Infant . . . infant] Female . . . female *MS. 1st rdg. del.*

Silent, silent Night

> Silent, silent Night,
> Quench the holy light
> Of thy torches bright;
>
> For possess'd of Day,
> Thousand spirits stray   5
> That sweet joys betray.
>
> Why should joys be sweet
> Usèd with deceit,
> Nor with sorrows meet?
>
> But an honest joy   10
> Does itself destroy
> For a harlot coy.

¹ fear'd the fury of my wind

> I fear'd the fury of my wind
> Would blight all blossoms fair and true;
> And my sun it shin'd and shin'd,
> And my wind it never blew.
>
> But a blossom fair or true   5
> Was not found on any tree;
> For all blossoms grew and grew
> Fruitless, false, tho' fair to see.

I fear'd, &c.] 1 I feared the roughness *MS. 1st rdg. del.*   4 And] But *MS. 1st rdg. del.*

Infant Sorrow

Infant Sorrow

i

My mother groan'd, my father wept;
Into the dangerous world I leapt,
Helpless, naked, piping loud,
Like a fiend hid in a cloud.

ii

Struggling in my father's hands,   5
Striving against my swaddling-bands,
Bound and weary, I thought best
To sulk upon my mother's breast.

iii

When I saw that rage was vain,
And to sulk would nothing gain,   10
Turning many a trick and wile
I began to soothe and smile.

iv

And I sooth'd day after day,
Till upon the ground I stray;
And I smil'd night after night,   15
Seeking only for delight.

v

And I saw before me shine
Clusters of the wand'ring vine;
And, beyond, a Myrtle-tree
Stretch'd its blossoms out to me.   20

Infant Sorrow] The two opening stanzas of this poem were later engraved
by Blake as one of the *Songs of Experience.* Cp. also another treatment of
the same theme in the first version of the 'Myrtle', which follows on the next
blank leaf of the *MS. Book.*   11 I began to trick and wile *MS.* 1*st rdg.
del.*; Seeking many an artful wile *MS.* 2*nd rdg. del.*   13 sooth'd]
grew *MS.* 1*st rdg. del.*; smil'd *MS.* 2*nd rdg. del.*   15 smil'd] grew *MS.*
1*st rdg. del.*   17 From this point onwards I give in the text the earlier

vi

But a Priest with holy look,
In his hands a holy book,
Pronouncèd curses on his head
Who the fruits or blossoms shed.

vii

I beheld the Priest by night;   25
He embrac'd my Myrtle bright:
I beheld the Priest by day,
Where beneath my vines he lay.

viii

Like a serpent in the day
Underneath my vines he lay: 30
Like a serpent in the night
He embrac'd my Myrtle bright.

ix

So I smote him, and his gore
Stain'd the roots my Myrtle bore;
But the time of youth is fled,   35
And grey hairs are on my head.

and preferable form of the remaining stanzas. Stanza v originally began
with the cancelled couplet:

> But upon the earthly ground
> No delight was to be found.

21 But a Priest] My father then *MS. and rdg.*   29-32 The two couplets of
this stanza were at first written in reversed order.

v–ix These last five stanzas were afterwards altered to the following
form, most of the changes being dependent upon the substitution of 'many
a Priest' for 'a Priest' in stanza vi:

> And I saw before me shine
> Clusters of the wand'ring vine;
> And many a lovely flower and tree
> Stretch'd their blossoms out to me.

Why should I care for the men of Thames

Why should I care for the men of Thames,
Or the cheating waves of charter'd streams ;
Or shrink at the little blasts of fear
That the hireling blows into my ear?

Tho' born on the cheating banks of Thames,   5
Tho' his waters bathèd my infant limbs,
The Ohio shall wash his stains from me :
I was born a slave, but I go to be free !

But many a Priest with holy look,
In their hands a holy book,
Pronounc'd curses on my head
And bound me in a myrtle shade.

I beheld the Priests by night ;
They embrac'd the blossoms bright :
I beheld the Priests by day ;
Underneath the vines they lay.

Like to holy men by day
Underneath the vines they lay :
Like to serpents in the night
They embrac'd my myrtle bright.

So I smote them, and their gore
Stain'd the roots my myrtle bore ;
But the time of youth is fled,
And grey hairs are on my head.

Why should I care, &c.] 7 I spurn'd his waters away from me *MS. 1st
rdg. del.*   8 I go to be free] I long to be free *MS. 1st rdg. del.*

Thou hast a lap full of seed

> Thou hast a lap full of seed,
> And this is a fine country.
> Why dost thou not cast thy seed,
> And live in it merrily?
>
> Shall I cast it on the sand   5
> And turn it into fruitful land?
> For on no other ground
> Can I sow my seed,
> Without tearing up
> Some stinking weed.   10

In a Myrtle Shade

> Why should I be bound to thee,
> O my lovely Myrtle-tree?
> Love, free Love, cannot be bound
> To any tree that grows on ground.
>
> O! how sick and weary I   5
> Underneath my Myrtle lie;
> Like to dung upon the ground,
> Underneath my Myrtle bound.
>
> Oft my Myrtle sigh'd in vain
> To behold my heavy chain: 10
> Oft my Father saw us sigh,
> And laugh'd at our simplicity.

Thou hast a lap full of seed] Cp. *Ahania*, chap. v, stanza 12 (p. 348 of this ed.).   5, 6 Shall I . . . turn] Oft I've . . . turn'd *MS. 1st rdg. del.*   7 For] But *MS. 1st rdg. del.*   9 tearing] pulling *MS. 1st rdg. del.*

In a Myrtle Shade] 5-8 This stanza, an afterthought, marked for insertion in its present position, began with the couplet afterwards deleted:

> To a lovely myrtle bound,
> Blossoms show'ring all around.

11 Oft the priest beheld us sigh *MS. 1st rdg. del.*

In a Myrtle Shade

So I smote him, and his gore
Stain'd the roots my Myrtle bore.
But the time of youth is fled,   16
And grey hairs are on my head.

To my Myrtle

To a lovely Myrtle bound,
Blossoms show'ring all around,
O how sick and weary I
Underneath my Myrtle lie!
Why should I be bound to thee,   5
O my lovely Myrtle-tree?

13-16 This stanza is identical with the final stanza of 'Infant Sorrow'.
To my Myrtle] A revised version of the preceding   Thus in the *MS.
Book*, deleted lines being indicated by italics:

To my Mirtle

5 'Why should I be bound to thee   *1
6 O my lovely mirtle tree
Love free love cannot be bound
To any tree that grows on ground.
1 To a lovely mirtle bound   *5
2 Blossoms showring all around
Like to dung upon the ground
Underneath my mirtle bound
3 O how sick & weary I   *9
4 Underneath my mirtle lie.'

It will thus be seen that Blake began by transcribing, as it stood, the first
stanza of the earlier version, beginning his second stanza with the couplet
which he had rejected in the previous draft and adding—but in transposed
order—two accepted couplets of the same stanza.   He then struck out ll. *3,
*4 and *7, *8, prefixing marginal numbers in his usual manner to indicate the
position of the lines retained.   Blake's intention is perfectly plain; yet we
find all Blake's editors following Rossetti in restoring the deleted lines *3, *4,
and printing the poem as two four-line stanzas.

To Nobodaddy

Why art thou silent and invisible,
Father of Jealousy?
Why dost thou hide thyself in clouds
From every searching eye?

Why darkness and obscurity   5
In all thy words and laws,
That none dare eat the fruit but from
The wily Serpent's jaws?
Or is it because secrecy gains females' loud applause?

Are not the joys of morning sweeter

Are not the joys of morning sweeter
Than the joys of night?
And are the vigorous joys of youth
Ashamèd of the light?

Let age and sickness silent rob   5
The vineyards in the night;
But those who burn with vigorous youth
Pluck fruits before the light.

Nobodaddy, a 'portmanteau word' for 'Nobody's Daddy', antithetical to
'Father of All', was Blake's jocular nickname for Urizen, the Father of
Jealousy. The same name occurs in 'Lafayette' (p. 123) and 'When Klop-
stock England defied' (p. 132). 2 Father] Man *MS. 1st rdg. del.* 9 females'
loud] feminine *MS. 1st rdg. del.* This line is an afterthought, added in
pencil.

Are not the joys, &c.] Cp. *Visions of the Daughters of Albion*, f. 6, ll. 5-7
(p. 290 of this ed.):

Innocence! honest, open, seeking
The vigorous joys of morning light, open to virgin bliss,
Who taught thee modesty, subtil modesty, child of night and sleep?

The Wild Flower's Song

The Wild Flower's Song

As I wander'd the forest,
The green leaves among,
I heard a Wild Flower
Singing a song.

'I slept in the earth   5
In the silent night,
I murmur'd my fears
And I felt delight.

'In the morning I went,
As rosy as morn,   10
To seek for new joy;
But I met with scorn.'

Day

The sun arises in the East,
Cloth'd in robes of blood and gold;
Swords and spears and wrath increas'd
All around his bosom roll'd,
Crown'd with warlike fires and raging desires.   5

The Wild Flower's Song] As originally written stanzas ii and iii formed
the entire poem. Later, on another page, Blake added the introductory
stanza, with the catchwords ('I slept in the Earth (*dark* del.) &c.') and
finally the title.   3 flower] thistle *MS. 1st rdg. del.*   5 I was found in
the dark *MS. 1st rdg. del.*

Day] 1 The day arises *MS. 1st rdg. del.*   4 bosom] ancles *MS. 1st
rdg. del.*

The Fairy

'Come hither, my Sparrows,
My little arrows.
If a tear or a smile
Will a man beguile,
If an amorous delay   5
Clouds a sunshiny day,
If the step of a foot
Smites the heart to its root,
'Tis the marriage-ring—
Makes each fairy a king.'   10

So a Fairy sung.
From the leaves I sprung;
He leap'd from the spray
To flee away;
But in my hat caught,   15
He soon shall be taught.
Let him laugh, let him cry,
He's my Butterfly;
For I've pull'd out the sting
Of the marriage-ring.   20

The Fairy] Blake's first title (afterwards erased) was 'The Marriage
Ring'. With these lines compare the proem to *Europe* (p. 303), and Blake's
sketch of the same subject in the *MS. Book*, afterwards engraved as one of
the plates of *The Gates of Paradise*. See also the poem on p. 127   7 step]
tread *MS.* 1st rdg. del.   19, 20 Originally written:

And the marriage ring
[*a line erased.*   ]

Motto to the Songs

Motto to the Songs of Innocence and of Experience

The Good are attracted by men's perceptions,
And think not for themselves ;
Till Experience teaches them to catch
And to cage the fairies and elves.

And then the Knave begins to snarl,   5
And the Hypocrite to howl ;
And all his good friends show their private ends,
And the eagle is known from the owl.

[Lafayette]

i

' Let the brothels of Paris be openèd
With many an alluring dance,
To awake the physicians thro' the city ! '
Said the beautiful Queen of France.

ii

The King awoke on his couch of gold,   5
As soon as he heard these tidings told :
' Arise and come, both fife and drum,
And the famine shall eat both crust and crumb.'

Motto] This motto, which was probably never engraved by Blake, is not
found in any copy of the *Songs*.

Lafayette] Written upon two opposite pages of the *MS. Book*, and
apparently abandoned unfinished. As it there stands, the rough draft
exhibits a bewildering series of erasures, corrections, re-writings, and
re-arrangements of lines into stanzas, and stanzas into various sequences,
dealt with in detail in my previous edition of the *Poems*. In the present
text I have attempted to give, so far as it can be ascertained, the last form
and order of the stanzas as indicated by Blake's final revisions, with the
earlier readings in footnotes.   3 physicians] pestilence *MS. 1st rdg. del.*
8 famine] *MS. 1st rdg. del.* ; but no word substituted.   ii Followed in
the MS. by the two erased stanzas :

Then old Nobodaddy aloft
. . . and belched and cough'd,

iii

The Queen of France just touch'd this globe,
And the pestilence darted from her robe;   10
But our good Queen quite grows to the ground,
And a great many suckers grow all around.

iv

Fayette beside King Lewis stood;
He saw him sign his hand;
And soon he saw the famine rage   15
About the fruitful land.

v

Fayette beheld the Queen to smile
And wink her lovely eye;
And soon he saw the pestilence
From street to street to fly.   20

And said 'I love hanging and drawing and quartering
Every bit as well as war and slaughtering.
Damn praying and singing,
Unless they will bring in
The blood of ten thousand by fighting or swinging!'

Then he swore a great and solemn oath ·
'To kill the people I am loth;
But if they rebel, they must go to hell:
They shall have a priest and a passing bell.'

These were later compressed into a single stanza, afterwards cancelled:

Then he swore a great and solemn oath:
'To kill the people I am loth,'
And said 'I love hanging and drawing and quartering
Every bit as well as war and slaughtering.'

11, 12 But the bloodthirsty people across the water
Will not submit to the gibbet and halter.   *MS. 1st rdg. del.*

12 There is just such a tree at Java found.   *MS. 2nd rdg. del.*

iv, v These two stanzas were afterwards cancelled.

Lafayette

vi

Fayette beheld the King and Queen
In curses and iron bound;
But mute Fayette wept tear for tear,
And guarded them around.

vii

Fayette, Fayette, thou'rt bought and sold   25
And sold is thy happy morrow;
Thou gavest the tears of pity away
In exchange for the tears of sorrow.

viii

Who will exchange his own fireside
For the stone of another's door?   30
Who will exchange his wheaten loaf
For the links of a dungeon-floor?

22 curses] tears *MS. 1st rdg. del.*
vii Afterwards cancelled.   The stanza originally stood:

> Fayette, Fayette, thou'rt bought and sold
> For well I see thy tears
> Of Pity are exchanged for those
> Of selfish slavish fears.

Then followed the deleted beginning of an unfinished stanza:

> Fayette beside his banner stood,
> His captains false around,
> Thou'rt bought and sold—

viii, ix These two stanzas are an expansion of the earlier version:

> Will the mother exchange her new-born babe
> For the dog at the wintry door?
> Yet thou dost exchange thy pitying tears
> For the links of a dungeon-floor!

30 stone] steps *MS. 1st rdg. del.*
32 Followed in the MS. by the erased lines:

> Who will exchange his own heart's blood
> For the drops of a Harlot's eye?

125

IX

O who would smile on the wintry seas
And pity the stormy roar?
Or who will exchange his new-born child
For the dog at the wintry door?

36 Cp. *Urizen*, f. 23, l. 2 (p. 328, l. 448 of this ed.).

APPENDIX

TO THE

EARLIER POEMS IN THE ROSSETTI MS.

A Fairy leapt upon my knee
Singing and dancing merrily ;
I said, ‘ Thou thing of patches, rings,
Pins, necklaces, and such-like things,
Disgracer of the female form,   5
Thou paltry, gilded, poisonous worm !’
Weeping, he fell upon my thigh,
And thus in tears did soft reply :
‘ Knowest thou not, O Fairies’ lord !
How much by us contemn’d, abhorr’d,   10
Whatever hides the female form
That cannot bear the mortal storm ?
Therefore in pity still we give
Our lives to make the female live ;
And what would turn into disease   15
We turn to what will joy and please.’

I place here a short poem printed by Swinburne in his *Essay* (pp. 143-4, *note*), who refers to it as ‘ copied from a loose scrap of paper, on the back of which is a pencilled sketch of Hercules throttling the serpents, whose twisted limbs make a sort of spiral cradle around and above the child’s triumphant figure : an attendant, naked, falls back in terror with sharp recoil of drawn-up limbs ; Alcmene and Amphitryon watch the struggle in silence, he grasping her hand.’

I have little doubt that this ‘ loose scrap of paper’ must have been one of those enclosed in, but not afterwards bound up with, the *MS. Book*, when it was acquired by D. G. Rossetti ; the piece itself in theme and manner closely resembling ‘ The Fairy’ in the preceding section, written *circa* 1793, and the proem to *Europe* engraved 1794.

POEMS FROM THE ROSSETTI MS.

II

Written *circa* 1800–1810

My Spectre around me night and day

i

    My Spectre around me night and day
    Like a wild beast guards my way;
    My Emanation far within
    Weeps incessantly for my sin.

My Spectre] Probably composed in October or November, 1800, soon after Blake's removal to Felpham, when he resumed the use of his old sketch-book as a notebook for poetry. The symbolism, which is identical with that of the revised version of *The Four Zoas*, Book VII, points also to the same date. Cp. also for very close parallelisms *Milton*, ff. 32 and *32 (quoted on p. 380 of this ed.).

This poem is another of those left in very rough draft by the author, and subjected to a great many changes and revisions, before the stanzas finally approved by him were numbered i–xiv. Later, however, around a sketch of Daphne in the middle of the page, he added four complementary stanzas: 'O'er my sins thou sit and moan', 'What transgressions I commit'—numbered respectively '1' and '2'—and an unnumbered stanza 'Poor, pale, pitiable form', followed by another which is now almost illegible. These stanzas, which like xiii and xiv are in pencil, were evidently intended for insertion in the poem, though Blake has not clearly indicated their precise position. The stanzas numbered '1' and '2' (in this ed. 'A', 'B') are undoubtedly part of the speech of the 'Emanation' or 'Jealous Female', and hence, it would seem, ought immediately to precede ix and x, which in the *MS. Book* stand at the head of the sheet, Blake's 1 and 2 perhaps being intended to signify that these stanzas take precedence of everything upon the same page.

Again, the unnumbered stanza beginning 'Poor, pale, pitiable form' (in this

My Spectre around me night and day

ii

'A fathomless and boundless deep,　　　　　　5
There we wander, there we weep ;
On the hungry craving wind
My Spectre follows thee behind.

iii

'He scents thy footsteps in the snow,
Wheresoever thou dost go,　　　　　　　　　10
Thro' the wintry hail and rain.
When wilt thou return again ?

ed. 'C'), is no less clearly part of the speech of the original speaker, the Man
in his 'divided' or fallen state, and hence, with the partially obliterated stanza
which follows it, ought, it may be presumed, to precede stanza **xi**, from
which point the poem proceeds straightforwardly to its conclusion. I have
accordingly incorporated stanzas A–C in the text in the position where they
should be read, preserving, however, Blake's numbering of the original
stanzas, and enclosing the supplementary ones within square brackets.

i Followed in the *MS. Book* by the two cancelled stanzas :

> Thy [1st rdg. *Her*] weeping thou [*she*] shall ne'er give o'er.
> I sin against thee [*her*] more and more ;
> And never will from sin be free
> Till she forgives and comes to me.
>
> Thou hast parted from my side :
> Once thou wast a virgin bride :
> Never shalt thou a true love [*lover*] find :
> My Spectre follows thee behind.

ii Originally written :

> A deep winter [*night*] dark and cold,
> Within my heart thou didst unfold ;
> A fathomless and boundless deep ;
> There we wander, there we weep.

This is followed by another deleted stanza :

> When my love did first begin,
> Thou didst call that love a sin :
> Secret trembling, night and day,
> Driving all my loves away.

iv

'Dost thou not in pride and scorn
Fill with tempests all my morn,
And with jealousies and fears   15
Fill my pleasant nights with tears?

v

'Seven of my sweet loves thy knife
Has bereavèd of their life.
Their marble tombs I built with tears,
And with cold and shuddering fears.   20

vi

'Seven more loves weep night and day
Round the tombs where my loves lay,
And seven more loves attend each night
Around my couch with torches bright.

vii

'And seven more loves in my bed   25
Crown with wine my mournful head,
Pitying and forgiving all
Thy transgressions great and small.

viii

'When wilt thou return and view
My loves, and them to life renew?   30
When wilt thou return and live?
When wilt thou pity as I forgive?'

a

['O'er my sins thou sit and moan:
Hast thou no sins of thy own?
O'er my sins thou sit and weep,   35
And lull thy own sins fast asleep.]

13 Dost] Didst *MS. 1st rdg. del.*   32 as I forgive] and forgive
MS. 1st rdg. del.   a With interchange of the first and second persons
the original draft reading throughout ' I ' for ' thou ', and ' thy ' for ' my '—in

My Spectre around me night and day

b

['What transgressions I commit
Are for thy transgressions fit.
They thy harlots, thou their slave;
And my bed becomes their grave.]   40

ix

'Never, never, I return:
Still for victory I burn.
Living, thee alone I'll have;
And when dead I'll be thy grave.

x

'Thro' the Heaven and Earth and Hell   45
Thou shalt never, never quell:
I will fly and thou pursue:
Night and morn the flight renew.'

c

['Poor, pale, pitiable form
That I follow in a storm;   50
Iron tears and groans of lead
Bind around my aching head.]

xi

'Till I turn from Female love
And root up the Infernal Grove,
I shall never worthy be   55
To step into Eternity.

other words these lines as at first conceived were spoken to and not by the
Emanation. Compare the converse change in stanza xi.   c Followed in
the MS. by the partially illegible but unerased stanza:

      And let [? us go] to the . . . . . [? day]
      With many pleasing wiles . . . . .
      [? The man] that does not love your [? wiles]
      Will never [? win back] your smiles.

51, 53 I] thou *MS. 1st rdg. del.*   52 root] dig *MS. 1st rdg. del.*

xii

'And, to end thy cruel mocks,
Annihilate thee on the rocks,
And another form create
To be subservient to my fate.   60

xiii

'Let us agree to give up love,
And root up the Infernal Grove;
Then shall we return and see
The worlds of happy Eternity.

xiv

'And throughout all Eternity   65
I forgive you, you forgive me.
As our dear Redeemer said:
"This the Wine, and this the Bread."'

When Klopstock England defied

When Klopstock England defied,
Uprose William Blake in his pride;
For old Nobodaddy aloft
    .. and belch'd and cough'd;
Then swore a great oath that made Heaven quake,   5
And call'd aloud to English Blake.
Blake was giving his body ease,
At Lambeth beneath the poplar trees.

57 And] And I *MS. 1st rdg. del.*

When Klopstock, &c.] Swinburne (*Critical Essay*, pp. 31–2) refers the
origin of this Rabelaisian *jeu d'esprit* to the passages from Klopstock
rendered into English by Hayley for Blake's benefit during the latter's stay
at Felpham in 1803 (Hayley's *Diary*, Mar. 26, 29); but the reference to
Lambeth, and the repetition of l. 4 in 'Lafayette', point rather to its having
been written about 1793.

From his seat then started he.
And turn'd him round three times three.   10
The moon at that sight blush'd scarlet red,
The stars threw down their cups and fled,
And all the devils that were in hell,
Answerèd with a ninefold yell.
Klopstock felt the intripled turn,   15
And all his bowels began to churn,
And his bowels turn'd round three times three,
And lock'd in his soul with a ninefold key; . . .
Then again old Nobodaddy swore
He ne'er had seen such a thing before,   20
Since Noah was shut in the ark,
Since Eve first chose her hellfire spark,
Since 'twas the fashion to go naked,
Since the old Anything was created. . . .

Mock on, mock on, Voltaire, Rousseau

Mock on, mock on, Voltaire, Rousseau;
Mock on, mock on; 'tis all in vain!
You throw the sand against the wind,
And the wind blows it back again.

And every sand becomes a gem   5
Reflected in the beams divine;
Blown back they blind the mocking eye,
But still in Israel's paths they shine.

The Atoms of Democritus
And Newton's Particles of Light   10
Are sands upon the Red Sea shore,
Where Israel's tents do shine so bright.

15 intripled] ninefold *MS. 1st rdg. del.*   16 churn] burn *MS. 1st rdg.
del.*   17 And . . . round] They turned around *MS. 1st rdg. del.*   18
Two partially illegible lines omitted here.   24 Six partially illegible lines
omitted here.

I saw a Monk of Charlemaine

i

I saw a Monk of Charlemaine
Arise before my sight:
I talk'd to the Grey Monk where he stood
In beams of infernal light.

ii

Gibbon arose with a lash of steel,   5
And Voltaire with a wracking wheel:
The Schools, in clouds of learning roll'd,
Arose with War in iron and gold.

I saw a Monk] The first draft of this piece, written without title in the *Rossetti MS.* not later than April 1803, consisted of fourteen stanzas, which Blake later separated into two poems 'To the Deists' in *Jerusalem*, and 'The Grey Monk' of the *Pickering MS.*, indicating the beginning of the latter by a line drawn above stanza v. In the version engraved for *Jerusalem*, where the length is reduced to seven stanzas, Blake's first change was to mark xii, xiii, and xiv for insertion after iv. He then wrote the revised version of xii:

> When Satan first the black bow bent
> And the Moral Law from the Gospel rent
> He forg'd the Law into a sword
> And spill'd the blood of Mercy's Lord—

adding in the margin the new stanza:

> Titus! Constantine! Charlemaine!
> O Voltaire! Rousseau! Gibbon! vain
> Your Grecian mocks [*mocks and iron* del.] and Roman sword
> Against this image of his Lord—

which (omitting the original xiii) is linked to xiv by the catchword 'A tear is, &c.' The stanzas thus rejected Blake converted into a second poem, which he transcribed into the *Pickering MS.*, with the title 'The Grey Monk'. This begins with the original fifth stanza, the line 'I see, I see, the Mother said' being changed to 'I die, I die, the Mother said'. The remaining stanzas (vi–xi) are arranged in the order of the *MS. Book*, with the interpolation of iv between v and vi, and xiv between x and xi, these two stanzas being common to both versions. ii Of this stanza we have the rejected variants:

I saw a Monk of Charlemaine

iii

'Thou lazy Monk,' they said afar,
'In vain condemning glorious War,   10
And in thy cell thou shall ever dwell.
Rise, War, and bind him in his cell!'

iv

The blood red ran from the Grey Monk's side,
His hands and feet were wounded wide,
His body bent, his arms and knees   15
Like to the roots of ancient trees.

v

'I see, I see,' the Mother said,
'My children will die for lack of bread.
What more has the merciless tyrant said?'
The Monk sat down on her stony bed.   20

vi

His eye was dry, no tear could flow;
A hollow groan first spoke his woe.
He trembled and shudder'd upon the bed;
At length with a feeble cry he said:

vii

'When God commanded this hand to write   25
In the studious hours of deep midnight,
He told me that all I wrote should prove
The bane of all that on Earth I love.

Gibbon plied his lash of steel,
Voltaire turned his wracking wheel,
Charlemaine and his barons bold
Stood by, and mocked in iron and gold.

and

The wheel of Voltaire whirl'd on high,
Gibbon aloud his lash does ply,
Charlemaine and his clouds of war [*and his barons bold* 1st rdg. del.]
Muster around the Polar Star.

> 9, 10 'Seditious Monk' said Charlemaine,
> 'The glory of War thou condemn'st in vain,'
>
> *MS.* 1st rdg. del.

viii

'My brother starv'd between two walls;
Thy children's cry my soul appals: 30
I mock'd at the wrack and griding chain;
My bent body mocks at their torturing pain.

ix

'Thy father drew his sword in the North;
With his thousands strong he is [marchèd] forth;
Thy brother has armèd himself in steel   35
To revenge the wrongs thy children feel.

x

'But vain the sword and vain the bow,
They never can work War's overthrow,
The hermit's prayer and the widow's tear
Alone can free the world from fear.   40

xi

'The hand of Vengeance sought the bed
To which the purple tyrant fled;
The iron hand crush'd the tyrant's head,
And became a tyrant in his stead.

xii

'Until the tyrant himself relent,   45
The tyrant who first the black bow bent,
Slaughter shall heap the bloody plain:
Resistance and War is the tyrant's gain.

34 marchèd] deleted in MS. but no word substituted.   44 And usurped
the tyrant's throne and bed MS. 1st rdg. del.   xii Rewritten later in the
form adopted in *Jerusalem*.

I saw a Monk of Charlemaine

xiii

'But the tear of love—and forgiveness sweet,
And submission to death beneath his feet—   50
The tear shall melt the sword of steel,
And every wound it has made shall heal.

xiv

'For the tear is an intellectual thing,
And a sigh is the sword of an Angel King,
And the bitter groan of the martyr's woe   55
Is an arrow from the Almighty's bow.'

Morning

To find the Western path,
Right thro' the Gates of Wrath
I urge my way;
Sweet Mercy leads me on
With soft repentant moan: 5
I see the break of day.

The war of swords and spears,
Melted by dewy tears,
Exhales on high;
The Sun is freed from fears,   10
And with soft grateful tears
Ascends the sky.

---

xiii Omitted in both the *Jerusalem* and *Pickering MS*. versions.   55 of
the martyr's woe] for another's woe *MS. 1st rdg. del.*
Morning] 4–6 Or (since the original is without punctuation, *quaere* read:

> Sweet Mercy leads me on;
> With soft repentant moan
> I see the break of day.

It may also here be pointed out that the accuracy of Mr. W. A. White's
reading 'Mercy' for 'Morning' of all previous editors is confirmed by the
diagram on f. 54 of *Jerusalem*, where 'Reason', 'Desire', 'Wrath', 'Pity',
are arranged as North, South, East, and West around 'This World'.

Poems from the Rossetti MS.

The Birds

He. Where thou dwellest, in what grove,
 Tell me Fair One, tell me Love;
 Where thou thy charming nest dost build,
 O thou pride of every field!

She. Yonder stands a lonely tree,   5
 There I live and mourn for thee;
 Morning drinks my silent tear,
 And evening winds my sorrow bear.

He. O thou summer's harmony,
 I have liv'd and mourn'd for thee;   10
 Each day I mourn along the wood,
 And night hath heard my sorrows loud.

She. Dost thou truly long for me?
 And am I thus sweet to thee?
 Sorrow now is at an end,   15
 O my Lover and my Friend!

He. Come, on wings of joy we'll fly
 To where my bower hangs on high;
 Come, and make thy calm retreat
 Among green leaves and blossoms sweet.   20

You don't believe

You don't believe—I won't attempt to make ye:
You are asleep—I won't attempt to wake ye.
Sleep on! sleep on! while in your pleasant dreams
Of Reason you may drink of Life's clear streams.
Reason and Newton, they are quite two things;   5
For so the swallow and the sparrow sings.

1 You don't believe I would attempt to make ye. *MS. 1st rdg. del.*

You don't believe

Reason says 'Miracle': Newton says 'Doubt.'
Aye! that's the way to make all Nature out.
'Doubt, doubt, and don't believe without experiment':
That is the very thing that Jesus meant,   10
When He said 'Only believe! believe and try!
Try, try, and never mind the reason why!'

If it is true what the Prophets write

If it is true, what the Prophets write,
That the heathen gods are all stocks and stones,
Shall we, for the sake of being polite,
Feed them with the juice of our marrow-bones?

And if Bezaleel and Aholiab drew   5
What the finger of God pointed to their view,
Shall we suffer the Roman and Grecian rods
To compel us to worship them as gods?

They stole them from the temple of the Lord
And worshipp'd them that they might make inspirèd art
    abhorr'd;   10

The wood and stone were call'd the holy things,
And their sublime intent given to their kings.
All the atonements of Jehovah spurn'd,
And criminals to sacrifices turn'd.

I will tell you what Joseph of Arimathea

I will tell you what Joseph of Arimathea
Said to my Fairy: was not it very queer?
'Pliny and Trajan! What! are you here?
Come before Joseph of Arimathea.
Listen patient, and when Joseph has done
'Twill make a fool laugh, and a fairy fun.'

If it is true, &c.] 10 And worshipp'd them to make, &c., *MS. 1st rdg. del.*

Why was Cupid a boy

> Why was Cupid a boy,
> And why a boy was he?
> He should have been a girl,
> For aught that I can see.
>
> For he shoots with his bow,   5
> And the girl shoots with her eye,
> And they both are merry and glad,
> And laugh when we do cry.
>
> And to make Cupid a boy
> Was the Cupid girl's mocking plan;   10
> For a boy can't interpret the thing
> Till he is become a man.
>
> And then he's so pierc'd with cares,
> And wounded with arrowy smarts,
> That the whole business of his life   15
> Is to pick out the heads of the darts.
>
> 'Twas the Greeks' love of war
> Turn'd Love into a boy,
> And woman into a statue of stone—
> And away fled every joy.   20

9-12 In the first draft :
> Then to make Cupid a boy
> Was surely a woman's plan,
> For a boy ne'er learns so much
> Till he is become a man.

Now Art has lost its mental charms

' Now Art has lost its mental charms
France shall subdue the world in arms.'
So spoke an Angel at my birth;
Then said ' Descend thou upon earth;
Renew the Arts on Britain's shore,   5
And France shall fall down and adore.
With works of art their armies meet
And War shall sink beneath thy feet.
But if thy nation Arts refuse,
And if they scorn the immortal Muse,   10
France shall the arts of peace restore
And save thee from the ungrateful shore.'

Spirit who lov'st Britannia's Isle
Round which the fiends of commerce smile—

[*Cetera desunt*]

Now Art, &c.] Cp. a passage from Blake's *Advertisement* in the *MS. Book*:
' Let us teach Buonaparte and whomsoever else it may concern that it is not
Arts that follow and attend upon Empire, but Empire that attends upon and
follows the Arts.'   Also an annotation in his copy of Reynolds' *Discourses*,
p. cxxv : ' The foundation of Empire is Art and Science.   Remove them, or
degrade them, and the Empire is no more.   Empire follows Art, and not
vice versa as Englishmen suppose.'   12 And save thy works from
Britain's shore. *MS. 1st rdg. del.*

I rose up at the dawn of day

I rose up at the dawn of day—
'Get thee away! get thee away!
Pray'st thou for riches? Away! away!
This is the Throne of Mammon grey.'

Said I: This, sure, is very odd;   5
I took it to be the Throne of God.
For everything besides I have:
It is only for riches that I can crave.

I have mental joy, and mental health,
And mental friends, and mental wealth;   10
I've a wife I love, and that loves me;
I've all but riches bodily.

I am in God's presence night and day,
And He never turns His face away;
The accuser of sins by my side doth stand,   15
And he holds my money-bag in his hand.

For my worldly things God makes him pay,
And he'd pay for more if to him I would pray;
And so you may do the worst you can do;
Be assur'd, Mr. Devil, I won't pray to you.   20

I rose up, &c.] Written under and partly around an entry dated Aug.
1807. Cp. a note written upon a different page of the *MS. Book* in the earlier
part of the same year: 'Tuesday Jan⁷. 20, 1807, between two and seven
in the evening Despair.'   13-20 These two stanzas were a later addition.

I rose up at the dawn of day

Then if for riches I must not pray,
God knows, I little of prayers need say;
So, as a church is known by its steeple,
If I pray it must be for other people.

He says, if I do not worship him for a God, 25
I shall eat coarser food, and go worse shod;
So, as I don't value such things as these,
You must do, Mr. Devil, just as God please.

The Caverns of the Grave I've seen

The Caverns of the Grave I've seen,
And these I show'd to England's Queen.
But now the Caves of Hell I view,
Who shall I dare to show them to?
What mighty soul in Beauty's form   5
Shall dauntless view the infernal storm?
Egremont's Countess can control
The flames of Hell that round me roll;
If she refuse, I still go on
Till the Heavens and Earth are gone,   10
Still admir'd by noble minds,
Follow'd by Envy on the winds,
Re-engrav'd time after time,
Ever in their youthful prime,
My designs unchang'd remain.   15
Time may rage, but rage in vain.
For above Time's troubled fountains,
On the great Atlantic Mountains,
In my Golden House on high,
There they shine eternally.   20

The Caverns, &c.] Apparently dedicatory verses to accompany Blake's large water-colour painting of 'The Last Judgement', executed for the Countess of Egremont, being an elaboration of the earlier design for Blair's *Grave*, dedicated to Queen Charlotte. See Blake's description of this picture in a letter to Ozias Humphrey, dated 18th Feb., 1808 (*Letters*. ed. Russell, p. 198). These lines are found on a page of the *MS. Book* containing part of Blake's interpretative account of the work, headed 'For the Year 1810: Addition to Blake's Catalogue of Pictures, &c.'   1 Caverns] Visions *MS. 1st rdg. del.*   3 But] And *MS. 1st rdg. del.*   6 dauntless] dare to *MS. 1st rdg. del.*   7 can] dare *MS. 1st rdg. del.*   8 flames] doors *MS. 1st rdg. del.*   11 noble] worthy *MS. 1st rdg. del.*   15 unchang'd] shall still *MS. 1st rdg. del.*

ADDENDUM TO THE LATER POEMS IN THE ROSSETTI MS.

To the Queen

The Door of Death is made of gold,
That mortal eyes cannot behold;
But when the mortal eyes are clos'd,
And cold and pale the limbs repos'd.
The soul awakes; and, wond'ring, sees   5
In her mild hand the golden Keys:
The Grave is Heaven's Golden Gate,
And rich and poor around it wait;
O Shepherdess of England's fold,
Behold this Gate of Pearl and Gold!   10

To dedicate to England's Queen
The visions that my soul has seen,
And, by her kind permission, bring
What I have borne on solemn wing,
From the vast regions of the Grave,   15
Before her throne my wings I wave;
Bowing before my Sov'reign's feet,
'The Grave produc'd these blossoms sweet
  mild repose from earthly strife;
The blossoms of Eternal Life!'   20

To the Queen] This poem. Blake's Dedication to his Illustrations of Blair's *Grave* (published 1808), where it is printed in ordinary typography, may not unfitly be placed here in view of its close connection with the preceding lines, although it does not form part of the *Rossetti MS.*

POEMS FROM THE ROSSETTI MS.

III

Written *circa* 1810

THE EVERLASTING GOSPEL

a

The Vision of Christ that thou dost see
Is my vision's greatest enemy.
Thine has a great hook nose like thine ,
Mine has a snub nose like to mine.

We have no entire or fair copy of this poem, the text of which is pieced together from passages scattered throughout the *MS. Book*. As these were written for the most part on vacant spaces of pages already partially filled with the draft of his Catalogue 'for the year 1810', it is clear that 'The Everlasting Gospel' was composed not earlier (though probably not much later) than this date.

The poem consists of eight sections, here numbered α–θ, the sequence of which in most cases has been indicated by Blake himself. Of these, besides the Prologue α and the Epilogue θ, the sections β, γ and ζ appear to be complete. So too the section ε 'Was Jesus born of a Virgin pure', which though not written into the *MS. Book* itself, but on a folded scrap of paper now bound in at the end of the volume, has happily been preserved from loss. This passage has no place assigned to it by the author, but its natural position would seem to be immediately before ζ, where I print it in the present arrangement. Of the remaining sections δ and η we possess only the opening lines, presumably intended, according to Blake's usual practice, to serve merely as catchwords to passages copied in full elsewhere. Probably these, like ε, were written upon separate pieces of paper, loosely inserted in the *MS. Book*, and lost before D. G. Rossetti purchased the volume from Samuel Palmer.

Title] First written at the head of the revised version of γ.

Thine is the Friend of all Mankind;   5
Mine speaks in parables to the blind.
Thine loves the same world that mine hates :
Thy heaven doors are my hell gates.
Socrates taught what Meletus
Loath'd as a nation's bitterest curse,   10
And Caiaphas was in his own mind
A benefactor to mankind.
Both read the Bible day and night,
But thou read'st black where I read white.

β

Was Jesus gentle, or did He
Give any marks of gentility ?
When twelve years old He ran away,
And left His parents in dismay.
When after three days' sorrow found,   5
Loud as Sinai's trumpet-sound :
'No earthly parents I confess—
My Heavenly Father's business !
Ye understand not what I say,
And, angry, force Me to obey.   10
Obedience is a duty then,
And favour gains with God and men.
John from the wilderness loud cried ;
Satan gloried in his pride.
'Come,' said Satan, 'come away,   15
I'll soon see if you'll obey !
John for disobedience bled,
But you can turn the stones to bread.

β] 7, 8. In γ (l. 10) and ε (l. 34) Blake changed the last line of this couplet
to 'I am doing My Father's business'.

God's high king and God's high priest
Shall plant their glories in your breast,   20
If Caiaphas you will obey,
If Herod you with bloody prey
Feed with the sacrifice, and be
Obedient, fall down, worship me.'
Thunders and lightnings broke around,   25
And Jesus' voice in thunders' sound:
'Thus I seize the spiritual prey.
Ye smiters with disease, make way.
I come your King and God to seize,
Is God a smiter with disease?'   30
The God of this world rag'd in vain:
He bound old Satan in His chain,
And, bursting forth, His furious ire
Became a chariot of fire.
Throughout the land He took His course,   35
And trac'd diseases to their source.
He curs'd the Scribe and Pharisee,
Trampling down hypocrisy.
Where'er His chariot took its way,
There Gates of Death let in the Day,   40
Broke down from every chain and bar;
And Satan in His spiritual war
Dragg'd at His chariot-wheels: loud howl'd
The God of this world: louder roll'd
The chariot-wheels, and louder still   45
His voice was heard from Zion's Hill,
And in His hand the scourge shone bright;
He scourg'd the merchant Canaanite
From out the Temple of His Mind,
And in his body tight does bind   50
Satan and all his hellish crew;
And thus with wrath He did subdue
The serpent bulk of Nature's dross,
Till He had nail'd it to the Cross.

The Everlasting Gospel

He took on sin in the Virgin's womb   55
And put it off on the Cross and tomb
To be worshipp'd by the Church of Rome.

γ

Was Jesus humble? or did He
Give any proofs of humility?
Boast of high things with humble tone,
And give with charity a stone?
When but a child He ran away,   5
And left His parents in dismay.
When they had wander'd three days long
These were the words upon His tongue:
'No earthly parents I confess:
I am doing My Father's business.'   10
When the rich learnèd Pharisee
Came to consult Him secretly,
Upon his heart with iron pen
He wrote 'Ye must be born again.'
He was too proud to take a bribe;   15
He spoke with authority, not like a Scribe.
He says with most consummate art
'Follow Me, I am meek and lowly of heart,
As that is the only way to escape
The miser's net and the glutton's trap.   20
What can be done with such desperate fools
Who follow after the heathen schools?

55 womb] Followed in MS. by the cancelled line with which this section of the poem originally ended:

> But on the Cross he sealed its doom.

γ] On another page of the *MS. Book* we find Blake's first draft of this passage containing 38, or with marginal additions, 46 lines. The variant readings of this earlier version, which I refer to as γ', are given in the footnotes.   11-14 In γ' these two couplets were written in the reversed order.

149

I was standing by when Jesus died;
What I call'd humility, they call'd pride.
He who loves his enemies betrays his friends.   25
This surely is not what Jesus intends;
But the sneaking pride of heroic schools,
And the Scribes' and Pharisees' virtuous rules;
For He acts with honest, triumphant pride,
And this is the cause that Jesus died.   30
He did not die with Christian ease,
Asking pardon of His enemies:
If He had, Caiaphas would forgive;
Sneaking submission can always live.
He had only to say that God was the Devil,   35
And the Devil was God, like a Christian civil;
Mild Christian regrets to the Devil confess
For affronting him thrice in the wilderness;
He had soon been bloody Caesar's elf,
And at last he would have been Caesar himself,   40
Like Dr. Priestly and Bacon and Newton—
Poor spiritual knowledge is not worth a button!
For thus the Gospel Sir Isaac confutes:
'God can only be known by His attributes;
And as for the indwelling of the Holy Ghost,   45
Or of Christ and His Father, it's all a boast
And pride, and vanity of the imagination,
That disdains to follow this world's fashion.'
To teach doubt and experiment
Certainly was not what Christ meant.   50
What was He doing all that time,
From twelve years old to manly prime?

25 betrays] hates *MS.* 1st *rdg. del.*   26 surely is not] is surely not γ'.
Followed in γ' by the couplet:

> He must mean the mere love of civility
> And so He must mean concerning humility.

29 But He acts with triumphant, honest pride γ'.   30 cause that] reason γ'.
31-50 These lines are an addition.

Was He then idle, or the less
About His Father's business?
Or was His wisdom held in scorn   55
Before His wrath began to burn
In miracles throughout the land,
That quite unnerv'd the Seraph band?
If He had been Antichrist, Creeping Jesus,
He'd have done anything to please us;   60
Gone sneaking into synagogues,
And not us'd the Elders and Priests like dogs;
But humble as a lamb or ass
Obey'd Himself to Caiaphas.
God wants not man to humble himself: 65
That is the trick of the Ancient Elf.
This is the race that Jesus ran:
Humble to God, haughty to man,
Cursing the Rulers before the people
Even to the Temple's highest steeple,   70
And when He humbled Himself to God
Then descended the cruel rod.
' If Thou humblest Thyself, Thou humblest Me.
Thou also dwell'st in Eternity.
Thou art a Man: God is no more: 75
Thy own Humanity learn to adore,
For that is My spirit of life.
Awake, arise to spiritual strife,
And Thy revenge abroad display
In terrors at the last Judgement Day.   80

---

59 Antichrist, Creeping Jesus' a creeping Jesus *MS. 1st rdg. del.* For
this epithet compare a passage from a letter of Blake to Cumberland, dated
April 12, 1827 (Russell's ed., p. 222). 61 into synagogues] into the syna-
gogues γ'.   63 Not humble as a lamb or an ass γ'.   64 Obey'd] Obey γ'.
57–8   Humble toward God, haughty toward man
              This is the race that Jesus ran. γ'.

71 And] But γ'.   73 Why dost thou humble thyself to me γ' *1st rdg. del.*
76 Thy own] Thine own γ'.

God's mercy and long suffering
Is but the sinner to judgement to bring.
Thou on the Cross for them shalt pray—
And take revenge at the Last Day.'
Jesus replied, and thunders hurl'd :   85
' I never will pray for the world.
Once I did so when I pray'd in the Garden ;
I wish'd to take with Me a bodily pardon.'
Can that which was of woman born,
In the absence of the morn,   90
When the Soul fell into sleep,
And Archangels round it weep,
Shooting out against the light
Fibres of a deadly night,
Reasoning upon its own dark fiction,   95
In doubt which is self-contradiction ?
Humility is only doubt,
And does the sun and moon blot out,
Rooting over with thorns and stems
The buried soul and all its gems.   10
This life's five windows of the soul
Distorts the Heavens from pole to pole,

---

82 Is] Are γ'.   84 Whom thou shalt torment at the Last Day γ' rst rdg.
del.   85-8 These lines are an addition.   95, 96 Cp. *The Gates of Paradise*, 'The Keys of the Gates', ll. 13-15 :

> Two-horn'd reasoning, cloven fiction,
> In doubt which is self-contradiction,
> A dark Hermaphrodite, we stood.

97, 98 Cp. 'Auguries of Innocence,' ll. 109-10 (*Pickering MS.*, p. 174) :

> If the sun and moon should doubt.
> They'd immediately go out.

99 Cp *Jerusalem*, f. 43, l. 8 : 'If we are wrathful Albion will destroy Jerusalem with rooty groves.'   101, 102 Cp. the poem to *Europe*, ll. 1-6 (p. 303).

And leads you to believe a lie
When you see with, not thro', the eye
That was born in a night, to perish in a night,   105
When the soul slept in the beams of light.

δ

This was spoken by my Spectre to Voltaire, Bacon, &c.

Did Jesus teach doubt? or did He
Give any lessons of philosophy,
Charge Visionaries with deceiving,
Or call men wise for not believing? . .

ε

Was Jesus born of a Virgin pure
With narrow soul and looks demure?
If He intended to take on sin
The Mother should an harlot been,
Just such a one as Magdalen,   5
With seven devils in her pen.
Or were Jew virgins still more curs'd,
And more sucking devils nurs'd?
Or what was it which He took on
That He might bring salvation?   10
A body subject to be tempted,
From neither pain nor grief exempted;
Or such a body as might not feel
The passions that with sinners deal?

103-6 Cp. 'Auguries of Innocence', ll. 125-8 (*Pickering MS.*, p. 174):
>   We are led to believe a lie
>   When we see not thro' the eye,
>   Which was born in a night, to perish in a night,
>   When the soul slept in beams of light.

ε] 7, 8 Interlineated in MS.

Yes, but they say He never fell.   15
Ask Caiaphas ; for he can tell.—
' He mock'd the Sabbath, and He mock'd
The Sabbath's God, and He unlock'd
The evil spirits from their shrines,
And turn'd fishermen to divines ;   20
O'erturn'd the tent of secret sins,
And its golden cords and pins,
In the bloody shrine of war
Pour'd around from star to star,—
Halls of justice, hating vice,   25
Where the Devil combs his lice.
He turn'd the devils into swine
That He might tempt the Jews to dine ;
Since which, a pig has got a look
That for a Jew may be mistook.   30
" Obey your parents."—What says He ?
" Woman, what have I to do with thee ?
No earthly parents I confess :
I am doing My Father's business."
He scorn'd Earth's parents, scorn'd Earth's God,   35
And mock'd the one and the other's rod ;
His seventy Disciples sent
Against Religion and Government—
They by the sword of Justice fell,
And Him their cruel murderer tell.   40
He left His father's trade to roam,
A wand'ring vagrant without home ;
And thus He others' labour stole,
That He might live above control.
The publicans and harlots He   45
Selected for His company,

17–48 No quot. marks in MS.   21-4 A marginal addition.   24
Pour'd] Not legibly written in MS , perhaps ' Pass'd'.   25, 26 A later
marginal addition.   35 earth's God] his God MS. 1st rdg. del.

And from the adulteress turn'd away
God's righteous law, that lost its prey.'

5

Was Jesus chaste? or did He
Give any lessons of chastity?
The Morning blushèd fiery red:
Mary was found in adulterous bed;
Earth groan'd beneath, and Heaven above   5
Trembled at discovery of Love
Jesus was sitting in Moses' chair.
They brought the trembling woman there.
Moses commands she be ston'd to death.
What was the sound of Jesus' breath?   10
He laid His hand on Moses' law;
The ancient Heavens, in silent awe,
Writ with curses from pole to pole,
All away began to roll.
The Earth trembling and naked lay   15
In secret bed of mortal clay;
On Sinai felt the Hand Divine
Pulling back the bloody shrine;
And she heard the breath of God,
As she heard by Eden's flood: 20
'Good and Evil are no more!
Sinai's trumpets cease to roar!
Cease, finger of God, to write!
The Heavens are not clean in Thy sight.
Thou art good, and Thou alone;   25
Nor may the sinner cast one stone
To be good only, is to be
A God or else a Pharisee.

〔〕 27, 28 A marginal addition.

Thou Angel of the Presence Divine,
That didst create this Body of Mine,　　30
Wherefore hast thou writ these laws
And created Hell's dark jaws?
My Presence I will take from thee:
A cold leper thou shalt be.
Tho' thou wast so pure and bright　　35
That Heaven was impure in thy sight,
Tho' thy oath turn'd Heaven pale,
'Tho' thy covenant built Hell's jail,
Tho' thou didst all to chaos roll
With the Serpent for its soul,　　40
Still the breath Divine does move,
And the breath Divine is Love.
Mary, fear not! Let me see
The seven devils that torment thee.
Hide not from My sight thy sin,　　45
That forgiveness thou may'st win.
Has no man condemnèd thee?'
'No man, Lord.' 'Then what is he
Who shall accuse thee? Come ye forth
Fallen fiends of heavenly birth,　　50
That have forgot your ancient love,
And driven away my trembling Dove.
You shall bow before her feet;
You shall lick the dust for meat;
And tho' you cannot love, but hate,　　55
Shall be beggars at Love's gate.
What was thy love? Let Me see it;
Was it love or dark deceit?'
'Love too long from me has fled;
'Twas dark deceit, to earn my bread;　　60
'Twas covet, or 'twas custom, or
Some trifle not worth caring for;
That they may call a shame and sin
Love's temple that God dwelleth in,

And hide in secret hidden shrine   65
The naked Human Form Divine,
And render that a lawless thing
On which the Soul expands its wing.
But this, O Lord, this was my sin,
When first I let these devils in,   70
In dark pretence to chastity
Blaspheming Love, blaspheming Thee,
Thence rose secret adulteries,
And thence did covet also rise.
My sin Thou hast forgiven me;   75
Canst Thou forgive my blasphemy?
Canst Thou return to this dark hell,
And in my burning bosom dwell?
And canst Thou die that I may live?
And canst Thou pity and forgive?'   80
Then roll'd the shadowy Man away
From the limbs of Jesus, to make them His prey,
An ever devouring appetite,
Glittering with festering venoms bright;
Crying 'Crucify this cause of distress,   85
Who don't keep the secrets of holiness!
The mental powers by diseases we bind;
But He heals the deaf, the dumb, and the blind.
Whom God has afflicted for secret ends,
He comforts and heals and calls them friends.'   90
But, when Jesus was crucified,
Then was perfected His galling pride.
In three nights He devour'd His prey,
And still He devours the body of clay;
For dust and clay is the Serpent's meat,   95
Which never was made for Man to eat.

65–8 An addition.   85–90 An addition.   93, 94 Cp. *Jerusalem*,
f. 89, l. 13:

      In three days He devour'd the rejected corse of death.
95, 96 A marginal addition.

η

Seeing this False Christ, in fury and passion
I made my voice heard all over the nation.
What are those . . .

θ

[Epilogue]

I am sure this Jesus will not do,
Either for Englishman or Jew.

η] The '&c.', which follows in the *MS.*, shows that the whole of the passage, of which these were the opening lines, must have been transcribed elsewhere. With l. 3 compare 'What are those Golden Builders doing', a line which occurs in *Jerusalem*, fol. 12, and again in fol. 27 of the same poem (pp. 387 and 391 of this edition).

THE PICKERING MANUSCRIPT

Circa 1801–1803

THE PICKERING MS.

The Smile

There is a smile of love,
And there is a smile of deceit,
And there is a smile of smiles
In which these two smiles meet.

And there is a frown of hate,   5
And there is a frown of disdain,
And there is a frown of frowns
Which you strive to forget in vain,

For it sticks in the heart's deep core
And it sticks in the deep backbone—   10
And no smile that ever was smil'd,
But only one smile alone,

That betwixt the cradle and grave
It only once smil'd can be;
And, when it once is smil'd,   15
There's an end to all misery.

The Golden Net

Three Virgins at the break of day:—
'Whither, young man, whither away?
Alas for woe! alas for woe!'
They cry, and tears for ever flow.

The Golden Net] In its present form this poem is a fair copy of a rough
draft in the *Rossetti MS.*, without title.

1 2 In the opening couplet Blake returns to his first version in the
Ross. MS., there afterwards altered to:

> Beneath the whitethorn's lovely may
> Three Virgins at the break of day.

tne initial line of which, perhaps inadvertently omitted, seems necessary to
explain the reference to 'the branches' in l. 10.   D. G. Rossetti, followed by
most editors, begins with a triplet.   3 Alas . . . woe] Alas for woe! alas
for woe! alas for woe! *Ross. MS.*

The one was cloth'd in flames of fire,   5
The other cloth'd in iron wire,
The other cloth'd in tears and sighs
Dazzling bright before my eyes.
They bore a Net of golden twine
To hang upon the branches fine.   10
Pitying I wept to see the woe
That Love and Beauty undergo,
To be consum'd in burning fires
And in ungratified desires,
And in tears cloth'd night and day   15
Melted all my soul away.
When they saw my tears, a smile
That did Heaven itself beguile,
Bore the Golden Net aloft,
As on downy pinions soft,   20
Over the Morning of my day.
Underneath the net I stray,
Now entreating Burning Fire
Now entreating Iron Wire,
Now entreating Tears and Sighs—   25
O! when will the morning rise?

The Mental Traveller

I travell'd thro' a land of men,
A land of men and women too;
And heard and saw such dreadful things
As cold earth-wanderers never knew.

6. 24 iron wire] sweet desire *Ross. MS. 1st rdg. del.*   7 tears and sighs]
sighs and tears *Ross. MS. 1st rdg. del.*   11 Followed in the *Ross. MS.* by
the deleted passage :

> Wings they had that soft enclose
> Round their body when they chose,
> They would let them down at will,
> Or make translucent . .

20 on] by *Ross. MS.*   21 Over] O'er *Ross. MS.*   23 Burning Fire] flaming
fire *Ross. MS.*   26 When, O when, will Morning rise *Ross. MS. 1st rdg. del.*

For there the Babe is born in joy   5
That was begotten in dire woe;
Just as we reap in joy the fruit
Which we in bitter tears did sow.

And if the Babe is born a boy
He's given to a Woman Old,   10
Who nails him down upon a rock,
Catches his shrieks in cups of gold.

She binds iron thorns around his head,
She pierces both his hands and feet,
She cuts his heart out at his side,   15
To make it feel both cold and heat.

Her fingers number every nerve,
Just as a miser counts his gold;
She lives upon his shrieks and cries,
And she grows young as he grows old.   20

Till he becomes a bleeding Youth,
And she becomes a Virgin bright;
Then he rends up his manacles,
And binds her down for his delight.

He plants himself in all her nerves,   25
Just as a husbandman his mould;
And she becomes his dwelling-place
And garden fruitful seventyfold.

An agèd Shadow, soon he fades,
Wandering round an earthly cot,   30
Full fillèd all with gems and gold
Which he by industry had got.

And these are the gems of the human soul,
The rubies and pearls of a love-sick eye,
The countless gold of the aching heart,   35
The martyr's groan and the lover's sigh.

33-36] Cp. *Gnomic Verses* xx (p. 197 of this ed.).

They are his meat, they are his drink;
He feeds the beggar and the poor
And the wayfaring traveller:
For ever open is his door.   40

His grief is their eternal joy;
They make the roofs and walls to ring;
Till from the fire on the hearth
A little Female Babe does spring.

And she is all of solid fire   45
And gems and gold, that none his hand
Dares stretch to touch her baby form,
Or wrap her in his swaddling-band.

But she comes to the man she loves,
If young or old, or rich or poor;   50
They soon drive out the Agèd Host,
A beggar at another's door.

He wanders weeping far away,
Until some other take him in;
Oft blind and age-bent, sore distrest,   55
Until he can a Maiden win.

And to allay his freezing age,
The poor man takes her in his arms;
The cottage fades before his sight,
The garden and its lovely charms.   60

The guests are scatter'd thro' the land,
For the eye altering alters all;
The senses roll themselves in fear,
And the flat earth becomes a ball;

The stars, sun, moon, all shrink away,   65
A desert vast without a bound,
And nothing left to eat or drink,
And a dark desert all around

The Mental Traveller

The honey of her infant lips,
The bread and wine of her sweet smile,   70
The wild game of her roving eye,
Does him to infancy beguile ;

For as he eats and drinks he grows
Younger and younger every day ;
And on the desert wild they both   75
Wander in terror and dismay.

Like the wild stag she flees away,
Her fear plants many a thicket wild ;
While he pursues her night and day,
By various arts of love beguil'd ;   80

By various arts of love and hate,
Till the wide desert planted o'er
With labyrinths of wayward love,
Where roam the lion, wolf, and boar.

Till he becomes a wayward Babe,   85
And she a weeping Woman Old.
Then many a lover wanders here ;
The sun and stars are nearer roll'd ;

The trees bring forth sweet ecstasy
To all who in the desert roam ;   90
Till many a city there is built,
And many a pleasant shepherd's home.

But when they find the Frowning Babe,
Terror strikes thro' the region wide :
They cry 'The Babe ! the Babe is born !'   95
And flee away on every side.

For who dare touch the Frowning Form,
His arm is wither'd to its root ;
Lions, boars, wolves, all howling flee,
And every tree does shed its fruit.   100

And none can touch that Frowning Form,
Except it be a Woman Old ;
She nails him down upon the rock,
And all is done as I have told.

The Land of Dreams

Awake, awake, my little boy !
Thou wast thy mother's only joy ;
Why dost thou weep in thy gentle sleep ?
Awake ! thy father does thee keep.

'O, what land is the Land of Dreams ?   5
What are its mountains, and what are its streams ?
O father ! I saw my mother there,
Among the lilies by waters fair.

' Among the lambs, clothèd in white,
She walk'd with her Thomas in sweet delight.   10
I wept for joy, like a dove I mourn ;
O ! when shall I again return ? '

Dear child, I also by pleasant streams
Have wander'd all night in the Land of Dreams ;
But tho' calm and warm the waters wide,   15
I could not get to the other side.

' Father, O father ! what do we here
In this lànd of unbelief and fear ?
The Land of Dreams is better far,
Above the light of the morning star.'   20

Mary

Sweet Mary, the first time she ever was there,
Came into the ball-room among the fair ;
The young men and maidens around her throng,
And these are the words upon every tongue :

Mary

'An Angel is here from the heavenly climes,   5
Or again does return the golden times;
Her eyes outshine every brilliant ray,
She opens her lips—'tis the Month of May.'

Mary moves in soft beauty and conscious delight,
To augment with sweet smiles all the joys of the night,   10
Nor once blushes to own to the rest of the fair
That sweet Love and Beauty are worthy our care.

In the morning the villagers rose with delight,
And repeated with pleasure the joys of the night,
And Mary arose among friends to be free,   15
But no friend from henceforward thou, Mary, shalt see.

Some said she was proud, some call'd her a whore,
And some, when she passèd by, shut to the door;
A damp cold came o'er her, her blushes all fled;
Her lilies and roses are blighted and shed   20

'O, why was I born with a different face?
Why was I not born like this envious race?
Why did Heaven adorn me with bountiful hand,
And then set me down in an envious land?

'To be weak as a lamb and smooth as a dove,   25
And not to raise envy, is call'd Christian love;
But if you raise envy your merit's to blame
For planting such spite in the weak and the tame.

'I will humble my beauty, I will not dress fine,
I will keep from the ball, and my eyes shall not shine;   30
And if any girl's lover forsakes her for me
I'll refuse him my hand, and from envy be free.'

21, 22 Cp. the lines in Blake's letter to Butts, dated Aug. 16, 1803:

O why was I born with a different face?
Why was I not born like the rest of my race?

She went out in morning attir'd plain and neat;
'Proud Mary's gone mad,' said the child in the street;
She went out in morning in plain neat attire, 35
And came home in evening bespatter'd with mire.

She trembled and wept, sitting on the bedside,
She forgot it was night, and she trembled and cried;
She forgot it was night, she forgot it was morn,
Her soft memory imprinted with faces of scorn; 40

With faces of scorn and with eyes of disdain,
Like foul fiends inhabiting Mary's mild brain;
She remembers no face like the Human Divine,
All faces have envy, sweet Mary, but thine;

And thine is a face of sweet love in despair, 45
And thine is a face of mild sorrow and care,
And thine is a face of wild terror and fear
That shall never be quiet till laid on its bier.

The Crystal Cabinet

The Maiden caught me in the wild,
Where I was dancing merrily;
She put me into her Cabinet,
And lock'd me up with a golden key.

This Cabinet is form'd of gold 5
And pearl and crystal shining bright,
And within it opens into a world
And a little lovely moony night.

Another England there I saw,
Another London with its Tower, 10
Another Thames and other hills,
And another pleasant Surrey bower,

The Crystal Cabinet

Another Maiden like herself,
Translucent, lovely, shining clear,
Threefold each in the other clos'd—   15
O, what a pleasant trembling fear !

O, what a smile ! a threefold smile
Fill'd me, that like a flame I burn'd ;
I bent to kiss the lovely Maid,
And found a threefold kiss return'd.   20

I strove to seize the inmost form
With ardour fierce and hands of flame,
But burst the Crystal Cabinet,
And like a weeping Babe became—

A weeping Babe upon the wild,   25
And weeping Woman pale reclin'd,
And in the outward air again
I fill'd with woes the passing wind.

The Grey Monk

'I die, I die !' the Mother said,
'My children die for lack of bread.
What more has the merciless tyrant said ?'
The Monk sat down on the stony bed.

The blood red ran from the Grey Monk's side,   5
His hands and feet were wounded wide,
His body bent, his arms and knees
Like to the roots of ancient trees.

The original draft of 'The Grey Monk' is found in the *Rossetti MS.*, where
it forms part of the poem beginning 'I saw a Monk of Charlemaine'. This
earlier version consisted of fourteen stanzas, which Blake afterwards
separated into two poems—transcribing nine stanzas, arranged in a slightly
different order and with some changes noted below, into the *Pickering MS.*,
under the title 'The Grey Monk', and engraving five, with two others added
later, as the untitled lines at the end of his 'Address to the Deists' (*Jerusalem,*
f. 52). Stanzas ii and viii of this version are common to all three poems.
1 I die, I die] I see, I see *Ross. MS.*   2 die] will die *Ross. MS.*   4 the
stony bed] her stony bed *Ross. MS.*

His eye was dry; no tear could flow:
A hollow groan first spoke his woe. 10
He trembled and shudder'd upon the bed;
At length with a feeble cry he said:

'When God commanded this hand to write
In the studious hours of deep midnight,
He told me the writing I wrote should prove 15
The bane of all that on Earth I love.

'My brother starv'd between two walls,
His children's cry my soul appalls;
I mock'd at the wrack and griding chain,
My bent body mocks their torturing pain. 20

'Thy father drew his sword in the North,
With his thousands strong he marchèd forth;
Thy brother has arm'd himself in steel,
To avenge the wrongs thy children feel.

'But vain the sword and vain the bow, 25
They never can work War's overthrow.
The hermit's prayer and the widow's tear
Alone can free the world from fear.

'For a tear is an intellectual thing,
And a sigh is the sword of an Angel King, 30
And the bitter groan of the martyr's woe
Is an arrow from the Almighty's bow.

'The hand of Vengeance found the bed
To which the purple tyrant fled;
The iron hand crush'd the tyrant's head, 35
And became a tyrant in his stead.'

15 the writing] that all *Ross. MS.*   20 mocks their] mocks at their
Ross. MS.   22 marchèd] is marched *Ross. MS.*   24 avenge] revenge
Ross. MS.   29 a tear] the tear *Ross. MS.*   33 found] sought *Ross. MS.*

Auguries of Innocence

    To see a World in a grain of sand,
    And a Heaven in a wild flower,
    Hold Infinity in the palm of your hand,
    And Eternity in an hour.
    A robin redbreast in a cage   5
    Puts all Heaven in a rage.
    A dove-house fill'd with doves and pigeons
    Shudders Hell thro' all its regions.
    A dog starv'd at his master's gate
    Predicts the ruin of the State.   10
    A horse misus'd upon the road
    Calls to Heaven for human blood.
    Each outcry of the hunted hare
    A fibre from the brain does tear.
    A skylark wounded in the wing,   15
    A cherubim does cease to sing.
    The game-cock clipt and arm'd for fight
    Does the rising sun affright.
    Every wolf's and lion's howl
    Raises from Hell a Human soul.   20
    The wild deer, wandering here and there,
    Keeps the Human soul from care.
    The lamb misus'd breeds public strife,
    And yet forgives the butcher's knife.
    The bat that flits at close of eve   25
    Has left the brain that won't believe.
    The owl that calls upon the night
    Speaks the unbeliever's fright.

The title 'Auguries of Innocence' probably, as Mr. Yeats conjectures, refers only to the opening quatrain, although the MS. itself has no space or line separating it from the couplets which follow. These proverbs are here placed in the sequence in which they appear in the MS., where they were doubtless transcribed from scattered jottings elsewhere. I append an attempt, made in my earlier edition of Blake, to rearrange them in an order which will enable the poem to be read as a whole, instead of as a series of disconnected distiches.

He who shall hurt the little wren
Shall never be belov'd by men.   30
He who the ox to wrath has mov'd
Shall never be by woman lov'd.
The wanton boy that kills the fly
Shall feel the spider's enmity.
He who torments the chafer's sprite   35
Weaves a bower in endless night.
The caterpillar on the leaf
Repeats to thee thy mother's grief.
Kill not the moth nor butterfly,
For the Last Judgement draweth nigh.   40
He who shall train the horse to war
Shall never pass the polar bar.
The beggar's dog and widow's cat,
Feed them, and thou wilt grow fat.
The gnat that sings his summer's song   45
Poison gets from Slander's tongue.
The poison of the snake and newt
Is the sweat of Envy's foot.
The poison of the honey-bee
Is the artist's jealousy.   50
The prince's robes and beggar's rags
Are toadstools on the miser's bags.
A truth that 's told with bad intent
Beats all the lies you can invent.
It is right it should be so ;   55
Man was made for joy and woe ;
And when this we rightly know,
Thro' the world we safely go.
Joy and woe are woven fine,
A clothing for the soul divine ;   60

37, 38 Cp. *The Gates of Paradise,* 'Keys of the Gates,' ll. 1, 2 :

> The caterpillar on the leaf
> Reminds thee of thy mother's grief.

Under every grief and pine
Runs a joy with silken twine.
The babe is more than swaddling-bands;
Throughout all these human lands
Tools were made, and born were hands,   65
Every farmer understands.
Every tear from every eye
Becomes a babe in Eternity;
This is caught by Females bright,
And return'd to its own delight.   70
The bleat, the bark, bellow, and roar
Are waves that beat on Heaven's shore.
The babe that weeps the rod beneath
Writes revenge in realms of death.
The beggar's rags, fluttering in air,   75
Does to rags the heavens tear.
The soldier, arm'd with sword and gun,
Palsied strikes the summer's sun.
The poor man's farthing is worth more
Than all the gold on Afric's shore.   80
One mite wrung from the labourer's hands
Shall buy and sell the miser's lands ·
Or, if protected from on high,
Does that whole nation sell and buy.
He who mocks the infant's faith   85
Shall be mock'd in Age and Death.
He who shall teach the child to doubt
The rotting grave shall ne'er get out.
He who respects the infant's faith
Triumphs over Hell and Death.   90
The child's toys and the old man's reasons
Are the fruits of the two seasons.
The questioner, who sits so sly,
Shall never know how to reply.

93 Cp. *Milton*, f. 43, ll. 12-17 (p. 381 of this ed.).

He who replies to words of Doubt   95
Doth put the light of knowledge out.
The strongest poison ever known
Came from Caesar's laurel crown.
Nought can deform the human race
Like to the armour's iron brace.   100
When gold and gems adorn the plough
To peaceful arts shall Envy bow.
A riddle, or the cricket's cry,
Is to Doubt a fit reply.
The emmet's inch and eagle's mile   105
Make lame Philosophy to smile.
He who doubts from what he sees
Will ne'er believe, do what you please.
If the Sun and Moon should doubt,
They'd immediately go out.   110
To be in a passion you good may do,
But no good if a passion is in you.
The whore and gambler, by the state
Licensed, build that nation's fate.
The harlot's cry from street to street   115
Shall weave Old England's winding-sheet
The winner's shout, the loser's curse,
Dance before dead England's hearse.
Every night and every morn
Some to misery are born.   120
Every morn and every night
Some are born to sweet delight.
Some are born to sweet delight,
Some are born to endless night.
We are led to believe a lie   125
When we see not thro' the eye,
Which was born in a night, to perish in a night,
When the Soul slept in beams of light.

126 When we see with, not thro' the eye *1st rdg. del.* Cp. 'Everlasting Gospel' γ, ll. 103–106 (p. 153 of this ed.).

God appears, and God is Light,
To those poor souls who dwell in Night; 130
But does a Human Form display
To those who dwell in realms of Day.

[*Editor's arrangement*]

To see a World in a grain of sand,
And a Heaven in a wild flower,
Hold Infinity in the palm of your hand,
And Eternity in an hour.

A robin redbreast in a cage
Puts all Heaven in a rage.
A dove-house fill'd with doves and pigeons
Shudders Hell thro' all its regions.
A dog starv'd at his master's gate
Predicts the ruin of the State.
A horse misus'd upon the road
Calls to Heaven for human blood.
Each outcry of the hunted hare
A fibre from the brain does tear.
A skylark wounded in the wing,
A cherubim does cease to sing.
The game-cock clipt and arm'd for fight
Does the rising sun affright.
Every wolf's and lion's howl
Raises from Hell a Human soul.
The wild deer, wandering here and there,
Keeps the Human soul from care.
The lamb misus'd breeds public strife,
And yet forgives the butcher's knife.
He who shall hurt the little wren
Shall never be belov'd by men.
He who the ox to wrath has mov'd
Shall never be by woman lov'd.
The wanton boy that kills the fly
Shall feel the spider's enmity.
He who torments the chafer's sprite
Weaves a bower in endless night.
The caterpillar on the leaf
Repeats to thee thy mother's grief.
Kill not the moth nor butterfly,
For the Last Judgement draweth nigh.

The Pickering MS.

He who shall train the horse to war
Shall never pass the polar bar.
The beggar's dog and widow's cat,
Feed them, and thou wilt grow fat.

The bat that flits at close of eve
Has left the brain that won't believe.
The owl that calls upon the night
Speaks the unbeliever's fright.
The gnat that sings his summer's song
Poison gets from Slander's tongue.
The poison of the snake and newt
Is the sweat of Envy's foot.
The poison of the honey-bee
Is the artist's jealousy.
A truth that 's told with bad intent
Beats all the lies you can invent.

Joy and woe are woven fine,
A clothing for the soul divine ;
Under every grief and pine
Runs a joy with silken twine.
It is right it should be so ;
Man was made for joy and woe ;
And when this we rightly know,
Thro' the world we safely go.

The babe is more than swaddling-bands;
Throughout all these human lands
Tools were made, and born were hands,
Every farmer understands.
Every tear from every eye
Becomes a babe in Eternity ;
This is caught by Females bright,
And return'd to its own delight.
The bleat, the bark, bellow, and roar
Are waves that beat on Heaven's shore.
The babe that weeps the rod beneath
Writes revenge in realms of death.
He who mocks the infant's faith
Shall be mock'd in Age and Death.
He who shall teach the child to doubt
The rotting grave shall ne'er get out.
He who respects the infant's faith
Triumphs over Hell and Death.

Auguries of Innocence

The child's toys and the old man's reasons
Are the fruits of the two seasons.
The questioner, who sits so sly,
Shall never know how to reply.
He who replies to words of Doubt
Doth put the light of knowledge out.
A riddle, or the cricket's cry,
Is to Doubt a fit reply.
The emmet's inch and eagle's mile
Make lame Philosophy to smile.
He who doubts from what he sees
Will ne'er believe, do what you please.
If the sun and moon should doubt,
They'd immediately go out.

The prince's robes and beggar's rags
Are toadstools on the miser's bags.
The beggar's rags, fluttering in air,
Does to rags the heavens tear.
The poor man's farthing is worth more
Than all the gold on Afric's shore.
One mite wrung from the labourer's hands
Shall buy and sell the miser's lands ;
Or, if protected from on high,
Does that whole nation sell and buy.
The soldier, arm'd with sword and gun,
Palsied strikes the summer's sun.
The strongest poison ever known
Came from Caesar's laurel crown.
Nought can deform the human race
Like to the armour's iron brace.
When gold and gems adorn the plough
To peaceful arts shall Envy bow.
To be in a passion you good may do,
But no good if a passion is in you.
The whore and gambler, by the state
Licensed, build that nation's fate.
The harlot's cry from street to street
Shall weave Old England's winding-sheet.
The winner's shout, the loser's curse,
Dance before dead England's hearse.

Every night and every morn
Some to misery are born.

Every morn and every night
Some are born to sweet delight.
Some are born to sweet delight,
Some are born to endless night.
We are led to believe a lie
When we see not thro' the eye,
Which was born in a night, to perish in a night,
When the Soul slept in beams of light.
God appears, and God is Light,
To those poor souls who dwell in Night;
But does a Human Form display
To those who dwell in realms of Day.

Long John Brown and Little Mary Bell

Little Mary Bell had a Fairy in a nut,
Long John Brown had the Devil in his gut;
Long John Brown lov'd little Mary Bell,
And the Fairy drew the Devil into the nutshell.

Her Fairy skipp'd out and her Fairy skipp'd in; 5
He laugh'd at the Devil, saying 'Love is a sin.'
The Devil he raged, and the Devil he was wroth,
And the Devil enter'd into the young man's broth.

He was soon in the gut of the loving young swain,
For John ate and drank to drive away love's pain; 10
But all he could do he grew thinner and thinner,
Tho' he ate and drank as much as ten men for his dinner.

Some said he had a wolf in his stomach day and night,
Some said he had the Devil, and they guess'd right;
The Fairy skipp'd about in his glory, joy and pride, 15
And he laugh'd at the Devil till poor John Brown died

Then the Fairy skipp'd out of the old nutshell,
And woe and alack for pretty Mary Bell!
For the Devil crept in when the Fairy skipp'd out,
And there goes Miss Bell with her fusty old nut. 20

Title] At first 'John Brown and Mary Bell'.   1, 3 Little] Pretty *1st*
rdg. del.   2, 3 Long] Young *1st rdg. del.*

William Bond

William Bond

I wonder whether the girls are mad,
And I wonder whether they mean to kill,
And I wonder if William Bond will die,
For assuredly he is very ill.

He went to church in a May morning,   5
Attended by Fairies, one, two, and three ;
But the Angels of Providence drove them away,
And he return'd home in misery.

He went not out to the field nor fold,
He went not out to the village nor town,   10
But he came home in a black, black cloud,
And took to his bed, and there lay down.

And an Angel of Providence at his feet,
And an Angel of Providence at his head,
And in the midst a black, black cloud,   15
And in the midst the sick man on his bed.

And on his right hand was Mary Green,
And on his left hand was his sister Jane,
And their tears fell thro' the black, black cloud
To drive away the sick man's pain.   20

' O William, if thou dost another love,
Dost another love better than poor Mary,
Go and take that other to be thy wife,
And Mary Green shall her servant be.'

'Yes, Mary, I do another love,   25
Another I love far better than thee,
And another I will have for my wife ;
Then what have I to do with thee?

'For thou art melancholy pale,
And on thy head is the cold moon's shine,
But she is ruddy and bright as day,
And the sunbeams dazzle from her eyne.'

30

Mary trembled and Mary chill'd,
And Mary fell down on the right-hand floor,
That William Bond and his sister Jane
Scarce could recover Mary more.

35

When Mary woke and found her laid
On the right hand of her William dear,
On the right hand of his loved bed,
And saw her William Bond so near,

40

The Fairies that fled from William Bond
Dancèd around her shining head;
They dancèd over the pillow white,
And the Angels of Providence left the bed.

I thought Love lived in the hot sunshine,
But O, he lives in the moony light!
I thought to find Love in the heat of day,
But sweet Love is the comforter of night.

45

Seek Love in the pity of others' woe,
In the gentle relief of another's care,
In the darkness of night and the winter's snow,
In the naked and outcast, seek Love there!

50

45-52 All editors place the last two stanzas in inverted commas, as though the speech were William Bond's. I treat it rather as that of the narrator of the story, who begins the poem in the first person.

POEMS

LETTERS

1800–1803

POEMS FROM LETTERS

To my dearest Friend, John Flaxman, these lines:

I bless thee, O Father of Heaven and Earth! that ever I saw
    Flaxman's face:
Angels stand round my spirit in Heaven; the blessèd of Heaven
    are my friends upon Earth
When Flaxman was taken to Italy, Fuseli was given to me for
    a season;
And now Flaxman hath given me Hayley, his friend, to be mine—
    such my lot upon Earth!
Now my lot in the Heavens is this: Milton lov'd me in childhood
    and show'd me his face;   5
Ezra came with Isaiah the Prophet, but Shakespeare in riper
    years gave me his hand;
Paracelsus and Behmen appear'd to me; terrors appear'd in the
    Heavens above;
The American War began; all its dark horrors pass'd before my
    face
Across the Atlantic to France; then the French Revolution
    commenc'd in thick clouds;
And my Angels have told me that, seeing such visions, I could
    not subsist on the Earth,   10
But by my conjunction with Flaxman, who knows to forgive
    nervous fear.

12 Sept., 1800.

For the setting of these poems see Mr. A. G. B. Russell's excellent
edition of *The Letters of William Blake*, 1906, to which I owe the correct text
of the first two pieces.

Poems from Letters

To my dear Friend, Mrs. Anna Flaxman

This song to the flower of Flaxman's joy,
To the blossom of hope for a sweet decoy;
Do all that you can, or all that you may,
To entice him to Felpham and far away.

Away to sweet Felpham, for Heaven is there;   5
The Ladder of Angels descends thro' the air;
On the turret its spiral does softly descend,
Thro' the village then winds, at my cot it does end.

You stand in the village and look up to Heaven;
The precious stones glitter on flights seventy-seven;   10
And my brother is there, and my friend and thine
Descend and ascend with the bread and the wine.

The bread of sweet thought and the wine of delight
Feed the village of Felpham by day and by night,
And at his own door the bless'd Hermit does stand,   15
Dispensing unceasing to all the wide land.

[To Thomas Butts]

To my friend Butts I write
My first vision of light,
On the yellow sands sitting.
The sun was emitting
His glorious beams   5
From Heaven's high streams.

To Anna Flaxman] In a letter dated 'H[ercules] B[uildings], Lambeth,
14 Sept., 1800,' the 'Hermit' being William Hayley, Blake's patron, who in
letters to his friends loved to refer to himself as the 'Hermit of Eartham' or
the 'Hermit of the Turret'. See also Blake's *Letters*, ed. Russell, *passim*.

To Thomas Butts] In a letter dated 'Felpham, Oct'. 2ᵈ, 1800', and addressed
to 'Mr. Butts, Great Marlborough Street'. These verses are prefaced by
the lines : 'Receive from me a return of verses such as Felpham produces by
me, tho' not such as she produces by her Eldest Son ; however, such as they
are, I cannot resist the temptation to send them to you.'

To Thomas Butts

Over sea, over land,
My eyes did expand
Into regions of air,
Away from all care;   10
Into regions of fire,
Remote from desire;
The light of the morning
Heaven's mountains adorning:
In particles bright,   15
The jewels of light
Distinct shone and clear.
Amaz'd and in fear
I each particle gazèd,
Astonish'd, amazèd;   20
For each was a Man
Human-form'd.   Swift I ran,
For they beckon'd to me,
Remote by the sea,
Saying: 'Each grain of sand,   25
Every stone on the land,
Each rock and each hill,
Each fountain and rill,
Each herb and each tree,
Mountain, hill, earth, and sea,   30
Cloud, meteor, and star,
Are men seen afar.'
I stood in the streams
Of Heaven's bright beams,
And saw Felpham sweet   35
Beneath my bright feet,
In soft Female charms;
And in her fair arms
My Shadow I knew,
And my wife's Shadow too,   40
And my sister, and friend.
We like infants descend

In our Shadows on earth,
Like a weak mortal birth.
My eyes, more and more,   45
Like a sea without shore,
Continue expanding,
The Heavens commanding;
Till the jewels of light,
Heavenly men beaming bright,   50
Appear'd as One Man,
Who complacent began
My limbs to enfold
In His beams of bright gold;
Like dross purg'd away   55
All my mire and my clay.
Soft consum'd in delight,
In His bosom sun-bright
I remain'd.   Soft He smil'd,
And I heard His voice mild,   60
Saying : 'This is My fold,
O thou ram horn'd with gold,
Who awakest from sleep
On the sides of the deep.
On the mountains around   65
The roarings resound
Of the lion and wolf,
The loud sea, and deep gulf.
These are guards of My fold,
O thou ram horn'd with gold !   70
And the voice faded mild :
I remain'd as a child ;
All I ever had known
Before me bright shone :
I saw you and your wife   75
By the fountains of life.
Such the vision to me
Appear'd on the sea.

To Mrs. Butts

To Mrs. Butts

Wife of the friend of those I most revere,
Receive this tribute from a harp sincere;
Go on in virtuous seed-sowing on mould
Of human vegetation, and behold
Your harvest springing to eternal life,   5
Parent of youthful minds, and happy wife!

[To Thomas Butts]

With Happiness stretch'd across the hills
In a cloud that dewy sweetness distils;
With a blue sky spread over with wings,
And a mild sun that mounts and sings;
With trees and fields full of fairy elves,   5
And little devils who fight for themselves—
Remem'bring the verses that Hayley sung
When my heart knock'd against the root of my tongue—
With angels planted in hawthorn bowers,
And God Himself in the passing hours;   10
With silver angels across my way,
And golden demons that none can stay;
With my father hovering upon the wind,
And my brother Robert just behind,
And my brother John, the evil one,   15
In a black cloud making his moan,—
Tho' dead, they appear upon my path,

To Mrs. Butts] These lines signed 'W. B.', which the author hopes
Mrs. Butts 'will excuse', conclude the letter from which the preceding poem
is taken.

To Thomas Butts] In a letter dated 'Felpham, Nov". 22, 1802', in which
Blake tells his correspondent that these lines 'were composed above a
twelvemonth ago, while walking from Felpham to Lavant to meet my sister'.

Notwithstanding my terrible wrath;
They beg, they entreat, they drop their tears,
Fill'd full of hopes, fill'd full of fears— 20
With a thousand angels upon the wind,
Pouring disconsolate from behind
To drive them off, and before my way
A frowning thistle implores my stay.
What to others a trifle appears 25
Fills me full of smiles or tears;
For double the vision my eyes do see,
And a double vision is always with me.
With my inward eye, 'tis an Old Man grey,
With my outward, a Thistle across my way. 30
'If thou goest back,' the Thistle said,
'Thou art to endless woe betray'd;
For here does Theotormon lour,
And here is Enitharmon's bower;
And Los the Terrible thus hath sworn, 35
Because thou backward dost return,
Poverty, envy, old age, and fear,
Shall bring thy wife upon a bier;
And Butts shall give what Fuseli gave,
A dark black rock and a gloomy cave.' 40

I struck the Thistle with my foot,
And broke him up from his delving root.
'Must the duties of life each other cross?
Must every joy be dung and dross?
Must my dear Butts feel cold neglect 45
Because I give Hayley his due respect?
Must Flaxman look upon me as wild,
And all my friends be with doubts beguil'd?
Must my wife live in my sister's bane,
Or my sister survive on my love's pain? 50
The curses of Los, the terrible Shade,
And his dismal terrors make me afraid.'

To Thomas Butts

So I spoke, and struck in my wrath
The Old Man weltering upon my path.
Then Los appear'd in all his power: 55
In the sun he appear'd, descending before
My face in fierce flames; in my double sight
'Twas outward a sun, inward Los in his might.
' My hands are labour'd day and night,
And ease comes never in my sight.   60
My wife has no indulgence given
Except what comes to her from Heaven.
We eat little, we drink less,
This Earth breeds not our happiness.
Another sun feeds our life's streams,   65
We are not warmèd with thy beams;
Thou measurest not the time to me,
Nor yet the space that I do see;
My mind is not with thy light array'd,
Thy terrors shall not make me afraid.'   70

When I had my defiance given,
The sun stood trembling in heaven;
The moon, that glow'd remote below,
Became leprous and white as snow;
And every soul of men on the earth   75
Felt affliction, and sorrow, and sickness, and dearth.
Los flam'd in my path, and the sun was hot
With the bows of my mind and the arrows of thought.
My bowstring fierce with ardour breathes;
My arrows glow in their golden sheaves;   80
My brothers and father march before;
The heavens drop with human gore.

Now I a fourfold vision see,
And a fourfold vision is given to me;
'Tis fourfold in my supreme delight,   85
And threefold in soft Beulah's night,

And twofold always.—May God us keep
From single vision, and Newton's sleep!

[To Thomas Butts]

O! why was I born with a different face?
Why was I not born like the rest of my race?
When I look, each one starts; when I speak, I offend;
Then I'm silent and passive, and lose every friend.

Then my verse I dishonour, my pictures despise,   5
My person degrade, and my temper chastise;
And the pen is my terror, the pencil my shame;
All my talents I bury, and dead is my fame.

I am either too low, or too highly priz'd;
When elate I'm envied; when meek I'm despis'd.   10

To Thomas Butts] In a letter dated 'Felpham, August 16, 1803', in which
Blake describes the circumstances which led to his trial for high treason.
Prefaced by: 'Give me your advice in my perilous adventure: burn what I
have peevishly written about my friend. I have been very much degraded
and injuriously treated; but, if it all arise from my own fault, I ought to blame
myself.'

1, 2] Cp. footnote to 'Mary', p. 167.

GNOMIC VERSES
EPIGRAMS

AND

SHORT SATIRICAL PIECES

Chiefly from

'THE ROSSETTI MANUSCRIPT'

(circa 1793–1810)

GNOMIC VERSES

I

Great things are done when men and mountains meet;
This is not done by jostling in the street.

To God
II

If you have form'd a circle to go into,
Go into it yourself, and see how you would do.

III

They said this mystery never shall cease:
The priest promotes war, and the soldier peace.

An Answer to the Parson
IV

Why of the sheep do you not learn peace?
Because I don't want you to shear my fleece.

Lacedaemonian Instruction
V

Come hither, my boy, tell me what thou seest there.
A fool tangled in a religious snare.

VI

Nail his neck to the cross: nail it with a nail.
Nail his neck to the cross: ye all have power over his tail.

Of the pieces in this section, all of which are taken from the *Rossetti MS.*, the greater number belong to the earlier entries and may be dated *circa* 1793. Another (no. XXII) would appear to have been written in 1806, while a few others—e. g. I, II, VI, XVIII, XIX, XXI, and XXIII—were probably composed between this date and 1810.

III 2 promotes] loves *MS. 1st rag. del.*

193

Gnomic Verses

VII

Love to faults is always blind ;
Always is to joy inclin'd,
Lawless, wing'd and unconfin'd,
And breaks all chains from every mind.

Deceit to secrecy confin'd,   5
Lawful, cautious and refin'd ;
To anything but interest blind,
And forges fetters for the mind.

VIII

There souls of men are bought and sold,
And milk-fed Infancy for gold ;
And Youth to slaughter-houses led,
And Beauty, for a bit of bread.

VII These companion stanzas are written at the head of two opposite pages
(106 and 107 reversed) of the *MS. Book.* I print them as one poem, their
connexion being obvious, though not indicated by Blake himself.   3 Law-
less, wing'd] Always wing'd *MS.* 1st *rdg.*, 'Always' being underlined, which
was probably a hasty attempt at erasure.

5–8 First written :

> Deceit to secrecy inclin'd,
> Modest, prudish and confin'd,
> Never is to interest blind,
> And chains in fetters every mind.

VIII Written immediately below the first stanza of the preceding piece, and
directly opposite to the first draft of stanza i of 'The Chimney Sweeper'.
As the latter comes below the lines 'Deceit to secrecy confin'd', it is not
unlikely that Blake here too wrote consecutive stanzas on blank spaces of
opposite pages, and hence that this quatrain was originally intended to form
part of 'The Chimney Sweeper'. See *Songs of Experience* (p. 104 of this ed.).
2 And cradled Infancy is sold *MS.* 1st *rdg. del.*   4 Beauty] Maidens
MS. 1st *rdg. del.*

Gnomic Verses

Soft Snow

> I walkèd abroad on a snowy day :
> I ask'd the soft Snow with me to play :
> She play'd and she melted in all her prime ;
> And the Winter call'd it a dreadful crime.

> Abstinence sows sand all over
> The ruddy limbs and flaming hair,
> But Desire gratified
> Plants fruits of life and beauty there.

Merlin's Prophecy

> The harvest shall flourish in wintry weather
> When two Virginities meet together :
> The king and the priest must be tied in a tether
> Before two Virgins can meet together.

> If you trap the moment before it 's ripe,
> The tears of repentance you'll certainly wipe ;
> But if once you let the ripe moment go,
> You can never wipe off the tears of woe.

> An Old Maid early ere I knew
> Aught but the love that on me grew ;
> And now I'm cover'd o'er and o'er,
> And wish that I had been a whore.

> O ! I cannot, cannot find   5
> The undaunted courage of a virgin mind ;
> For early I in love was crost,
> Before my flower of love was lost.

IX 4 Oh, that sweet love should be thought a crime ! *MS.* 1*st rdg. del.*
Cp. the introductory lines to ·A Little Girl Lost ' in the *Songs of Experience.*
   XII 1 trap] catch *MS.* 1*st rdg. del.*   4 You can] You'll *MS.* 1*st rdg. del.*

Gnomic Verses

XIV

The sword sung on the barren heath,
The sickle in the fruitful field:
The sword he sung a song of death,
But could not make the sickle yield.

XV

O lapwing! thou fliest around the heath,
Nor seest the net that is spread beneath.
Why dost thou not fly among the corn fields?
They cannot spread nets where a harvest yields.

XVI

Terror in the house does roar;
But Pity stands before the door.

XVII

Several Questions Answered

I

[Eternity]

He who bends to himself a Joy
Doth the wingèd life destroy;
But he who kisses the Joy as it flies
Lives in Eternity's sunrise.

2

The look of love alarms,   5
Because it's fill'd with fire;
But the look of soft deceit
Shall win the lover's hire.

---

xvii These five short pieces, the rough drafts of which are found on three
separate pages in the *MS. Book*, were afterwards transcribed by Blake in
their present form and sequence under the general title 'Several Questions
Answered'.   1–4 First written on another page with title 'Eternity'.
1 bends] binds *Max Plowman, conj.*   2 Doth] Does *MS. 1st draft*.
3 kisses] just kisses *MS. 1st draft, 1st rdg. del.*   4 Eternity's] an
eternal *MS. 1st draft, 1st rdg. del.*   6 it's] 'tis *MS. 1st draft*.

196

Gnomic Verses

3

Soft deceit and idleness,
These are Beauty's sweetest dress.   10

4

[The Question answered]

What is it men in women do require?
The lineaments of gratified desire.
What is it women do in men require?
The lineaments of gratified desire.

5

An ancient Proverb

Remove away that black'ning church,   15
Remove away that marriage hearse,
Remove away that man of blood—
You'll quite remove the ancient curse.

XVIII

If I e'er grow to man's estate,
O! give to me a woman's fate.
May I govern all, both great and small,
Have the last word, and take the wall.

XIX

Since all the riches of this world
May be gifts from the Devil and earthly kings,
I should suspect that I worshipp'd the Devil
If I thank'd my God for worldly things.

9, 10 Blake at first began this couplet with the line afterwards deleted :
Which are beauty's sweetest dress?
11–14 Title only in first draft.   11, 13 in] of *MS. 1st draft, 1st rdg. del.*
17 man] place *MS. 1st draft, 1st rdg. del.*   18 You'll] 'Twill *MS. 1st draft,
1st rdg. del.*

XX

Riches

The countless gold of a merry heart,
The rubies and pearls of a loving eye,
The indolent never can bring to the mart,
Nor the secret hoard up in his treasury.

XXI

The Angel that presided o'er my birth
Said 'Little creature, form'd of joy and mirth,
Go, love without the help of anything on earth.'

XXII

Grown old in love from seven till seven times seven,
I oft have wish'd for Hell, for ease from Heaven.

XXIII

Do what you will this life's a fiction,
And is made up of contradiction.

ON ART AND ARTISTS

I

Advice of the Popes who succeeded the Age of Raphael

Degrade first the Arts if you'd mankind degrade,
Hire idiots to paint with cold light and hot shade,
Give high price for the worst, leave the best in disgrace,
And with labours of ignorance fill every place.

---

xx 3 indolent] idle man *MS. 1st rdg. del.*   4 secret] cunning *MS. 1st rdg. del.*

xxi 2 form'd . . . mirth] thou art form'd for mirth *MS. 1st rdg. del.*

xxiii Written elsewhere in the *MS. Book* :

This corporeal life's a fiction
And is made up of contradiction.

On Art and Artists] Of the Epigrams grouped together in this section, written *circa* 1808–9, nos. I, V, XV, XXII, XXIV, XXX, XXXI, and XXXII are taken from

On Art and Artists

II

On the great encouragement given by English nobility and gentry to Correggio, Rubens, Reynolds, Gains-borough, Catalani, Du Crow, and Dilbury Doodle

As the ignorant savage will sell his own wife
For a sword, or a cutlass, a dagger, or knife;
So the taught, savage Englishman, spends his whole fortune
On a smear, or a squall, to destroy picture or tune;
And I call upon Colonel Wardle   5
To give these rascals a dose of caudle!

III

I ask'd my dear friend Orator Prig:
'What's the first part of oratory?' He said: 'A great wig.
'And what is the second?' Then, dancing a jig
And bowing profoundly, he said: 'A great wig.'
'And what is the third?' Then he snored like a pig,   5
And, puffing his cheeks out, replied: 'A great wig.'
So if a great painter with questions you push,
'What's the first part of painting?' he'll say: 'A paint-brush.'

Blake's marginal annotations to his copy of Vol. I of Sir Joshua Reynolds *Works* (2nd edition, 1798), containing the first eight 'Discourses'. Others occasioned by the six later 'Discourses' were jotted down in the *MS. Book*, whence also the remainder of the Epigrams and satirical pieces on Art and artists have been excerpted.

For prose parallelisms to the Epigrams readers may consult Blake's *Descriptive Catalogue*, the 'Advertisement', and 'Catalogue for 1810' from the *Rossetti MS.*, as well as the marginalia to Reynolds mentioned above, or refer to my earlier edition of the *Poems* where the more important of these illustrative passages have been quoted.

II Title: Du Crow] Pierre Ducros. Cp. Blake's *Letters*, ed. Russell, p. 204.
2 For a button, a bauble [buckle *2nd rdg. del.*], a bead, or a knife *MS. 1st rdg. del.*   3 taught] wise *MS. 1st rdg. del.*; learned *MS. 2nd rdg. del.*
4 On] For *MS. 1st rdg. del.*   to destroy] that is not *MS. 1st rdg. del.*
5 For Colonel Wardle see Hunt's *Examiner*, 1809, *passim*.

III Blake has marked this piece 'to come in *Barry: a Poem*'.   6 And, puffing his cheeks out,] And thrust out his cheeks and *MS. 1st rdg. del.*

'And what is the second?' with most modest blush,
He'll smile like a cherub, and say: 'A paint-brush.' 10
'And what is the third?' he'll bow like a rush,
With a leer in his eye, he'll reply: 'A paint-brush.'
Perhaps this is all a painter can want:
But, look yonder—that house is the house of Rembrandt!

IV

'O dear Mother Outline! of wisdom most sage,
What's the first part of painting?' She said: 'Patronage.'
'And what is the second, to please and engage?'
She frowned like a fury, and said: 'Patronage.'
'And what is the third? She put off old age, 5
And smil'd like a siren, and said: 'Patronage.

V

[On the Foundation of the Royal Academy]

When nations grow old, the Arts grow cold,
And Commerce settles on every tree;
And the poor and the old can live upon gold,
For all are born poor, aged sixty-three.

VI

These are the idiots' chiefest arts:
To blend and not define the parts
The swallow sings, in courts of kings,
That fools have their high finishings.

And this the princes' golden rule, 5
The laborious stumble of a fool.
To make out the parts is the wise man's aim,
But to loose them the fool makes his foolish game.

vi 3 The swallow sings] Let it be told *MS. 1st rdg. del*.

On Art and Artists

VII

The cripple every step drudges and labours,
And says : 'Come, learn to walk of me, good neighbours.'
Sir Joshua in astonishment cries out :
'See, what great labour ! pain in modest doubt !

'He walks and stumbles as if he crep,   5
And how high labour'd is every step !'
Newton and Bacon cry 'Being badly nurst,
He is all experiments from last to first.'

You say their pictures well painted be,
And yet they are blockheads you all agree :
Thank God ! I never was sent to school
To be flogg'd into following the style of a fool.
The errors of a wise man make your rule,   5
Rather than the perfections of a fool.

When you look at a picture, you always can see
If a man of sense has painted he.
Then never flinch, but keep up a jaw
About freedom, and 'Jenny sink awa'.'
As when it smells of the lamp, we can   5
Say all was owing to the skilful man ;
For the smell of water is but small :
So e'en let ignorance do it all.

VII 4 His pains are more than others, there's no doubt *MS. 1st rdg. del.*
VIII 4 To learn to admire the works of a fool *MS. 1st rdg. del.*
IX 4 Jenny sink awa'] i. e. 'Je ne sais quoi'.   5 we] all *MS. 1st rdg. del.*

On Art and Artists

X

The Washerwoman's Song

I wash'd them out and wash'd them in,
And they told me it was a great sin.

XI

English Encouragement of Art: Cromek's opinions put into rhyme

If you mean to please everybody you will
Set to work both ignorance and skill.
For a great multitude are ignorant,
And skill to them seems raving and rant.
Like putting oil and water in a lamp,   5
'Twill make a great splutter with smoke and damp.
For there is no use as it seems to me
Of lighting a lamp, when you don't wish to see.

XII

When I see a Rubens, Rembrandt, Correggio,
I think of the crippled Harry and slobbering Joe;
And then I question thus: Are artists' rules
To be drawn from the works of two manifest fools?
Then God defend us from the Arts I say!   5
Send battle, murder, sudden death, O pray!
Rather than be such a blind human fool
I'd be an ass, a hog, a worm, a chair, a stool!

x Possibly a reference to Blake's manner of using water-colour; cp. the allusion to 'water' in the preceding epigram.

xi I print here the earlier and clearer version of this piece, Blake's subsequent changes being noted below.   2 'Menny wouver' both bunglishness and skill *MS. 2nd rdg.*   5 putting] displaying *MS. 2nd rdg.*   6 'Twill make a great splutter] 'Twill hold forth a huge splutter *MS. 2nd rdg.*
7 For there is no use] For it's all sheer loss *MS. 2nd rdg.*   8 Of displaying up a light when we want not to see *MS. 2nd rdg.*

xii 1 When I see a Rembrandt or Correggio *MS. 1st rdg. del.*
3 question thus] say to myself *MS. 1st rdg. del.*   6 O] we *MS. 1st rdg. del.*

XIII

Give pensions to the learned pig,
Or the hare playing on a tabor;
Anglus can never see perfection
But in the journeyman's labour.

XIV

[On Sir Joshua Reynolds' disappointment at his first impressions of Raphael]

Some look to see the sweet outlines,
And beauteous forms that Love does wear;
Some look to find out patches, paint,
Bracelets and stays and powder'd hair.

XV

Sir Joshua praisèd Rubens with a smile,
By calling his the ornamental style;
And yet his praise of Flaxman was the smartest,
When he called him the ornamental artist.
But sure such ornaments we well may spare   5
As crooked limbs and lousy heads of hair.

XVI

Sir Joshua praises Michael Angelo.
'Tis Christian mildness when knaves praise a foe;
But 'twould be madness, all the world would say,
Should Michael Angelo praise Sir Joshua —
Christ us'd the Pharisees in a rougher way.   5

---

xv 6 Like a filthy infectious head of hair *MS. 1st rdg. del.* A crooked
stick and a lousy head of hair *MS. 2nd rdg. del.*

xvi 2 And counts it outrage thus to praise his foe *MS. 1st rdg. del.* 3 all
the world would] that we all must *MS. 1st rdg. del.* 5 This line added
later.

On Art and Artists

XVII

Can there be anything more mean,
More malice in disguise,
Than praise a man for doing what
That man does most despise?
Reynolds lectures exactly so   5
When he praises Michael Angelo.

XVIII

To the Royal Academy

A strange erratum in all the editions
Of Sir Joshua Reynolds' lectures
Should be corrected by the young gentlemen
And the Royal Academy's directors.

Instead of 'Michael Angelo,'   5
Read 'Rembrandt'; for it is fit
To make mere common honesty
In all that he has writ.

XIX

Florentine Ingratitude

Sir Joshua sent his own portrait to
The birthplace of Michael Angelo,
And in the hand of the simpering fool
He put a dirty paper scroll,
And on the paper, to be polite,   5
Did 'Sketches by Michael Angelo' write.
The Florentines said ''Tis a Dutch-English bore,
Michael Angelo's name writ on Rembrandt's door.'

xvii 3 what] that *MS. 1st rdg. del.*   4 That man] Which he *MS. 1st rdg. del.*   5 This Reynolds' lectures plainly shew *MS. 1st rdg. del.*

xviii 6–8   . . . . . and you will know
                 That Sir Joshua Reynolds now wished to speak
                 Of Michael Angelo.   *MS. 1st rdg. del.*

7 mere common] either sense or *MS. 1st rdg. del.*

On Art and Artists

The Florentines call it an English fetch,
For Michael Angelo never did sketch;   10
Every line of his has meaning,
And needs neither suckling nor weaning.
'Tis the trading English-Venetian cant
To speak Michael Angelo, and act Rembrandt:
It will set his Dutch friends all in a roar   15
To write 'Mich. Ang.' on Rembrandt's door;
But you must not bring in your hand a lie
If you mean that the Florentines should buy.
Giotto's circle or Apelles' line
Were not the work of sketchers drunk with wine;   20
Nor of the city clock's running . . . fashion;
Nor of Sir Isaac Newton's calculation.

XX

No real style of colouring ever appears,
But advertising in the newspapers.
Look there—you'll see Sir Joshua's colouring:
Look at his pictures—all has taken wing!

XXI

When Sir Joshua Reynolds died
All Nature was degraded;
The King dropp'd a tear into the Queen's ear,
And all his pictures faded.

XIX 18 Following this in the *MS. Book* are the lines :
> These verses were written by a very envious man,
> Who whatever likeness he may have to Michael Angelo
> Never can have any to Sir Jehoshuan.

19–22 These lines written later at foot of page. Another rdg. was :
> Nor of the city clock's idle facilities
> Which sprang from Sir Isaac Newton's great abilities.

XX 4 all has taken wing] 'tis quite another thing *MS. 1st rdg. del.*

On Art and Artists

A Pitiful Case   XXII

> The villain at the gallows tree,
> When he is doom'd to die,
> To assuage his misery
> In virtue's praise does cry.
>
> So Reynolds when he came to die,
> To assuage his bitter woe,
> Thus aloud did howl and cry:
> 'Michael Angelo! Michael Angelo!'

   5

XXIII

[On Sir Joshua Reynolds]

> O Reader, behold the Philosopher's grave!
> He was born quite a Fool, but he died quite a Knave.

XXIV

> I, Rubens, am a statesman and a saint.
> Deceptions [both]—and so I'll learn to paint.

XXV

[On the school of Rubens]

> Swelled limbs, with no outline that you can descry,
> That stink in the nose of a stander-by;
> But all the pulp-wash'd, painted, finish'd with labour,
> Of an hundred journeymen's—how-d'ye do neighbour?

XXVI

To English Connoisseurs

> You must agree that Rubens was a fool,
> And yet you make him master of your School,

XXII 7 did howl and] was heard to *MS. 1st rdg. del.*
XXIV   Rubens had been a statesman or a saint;
             He mixed them both—and so he learn'd to paint.
                                    MS. 1st rdg. del.

And give more money for his slobberings
Than you will give for Raphael's finest things.
I understood Christ was a carpenter
And not a brewer's servant, my good Sir.

5

XXVII

A Pretty Epigram for the encouragement of those who have paid great sums in the Venetian and Flemish ooze

Nature and Art in this together suit :
What is most grand is always most minute.
Rubens thinks tables, chairs and stools are grand,
But Raphael thinks a head, a foot, a hand.

XXVIII

Raphael, sublime, majestic, graceful, wise —
His executive power must I despise?
Rubens, low, vulgar, stupid, ignorant —
His power of execution I must grant,
Learn the laborious stumble of a fool !
And from an idiot's action form my rule?—
Go, send your Children to the Slobbering School !

XXIX

On the Venetian Painter

He makes the lame to walk, we all agree,
But then he strives to blind all who can see.

XXX

A pair of stays to mend the shape
Of crookèd humpy woman,
Put on, O Venus ; now thou art
Quite a Venetian Roman.

xxvii Title] A Pretty Epigram for those who have given high prices for
bad pictures *MS. 1st rdg. del.*

On Art and Artists

Venetian! all thy colouring is no more
Than bolster'd plasters on a crooked whore.

XXXII

To Venetian Artists

That God is colouring Newton does show,
And the Devil is a black outline, all of us know.
Perhaps this little fable may make us merry:
A dog went over the water without a wherry;
A bone which he had stolen he had in his mouth;   5
He cared not whether the wind was north or south.
As he swam he saw the reflection of the bone.
'This is quite perfection—one generalizing tone!
Outline! There's no outline, there's no such thing:
All is chiaroscuro, poco-pen—it's all colouring!'   10
Snap, snap! He has lost shadow and substance too.
He had them both before. 'Now how do ye do?'
'A great deal better than I was before:
Those who taste colouring love it more and more.'

XXXIII

All pictures that's painted with sense and with thought
Are painted by madmen, as sure as a groat;
For the greater the fool is the pencil more blest,
As when they are drunk they always paint best.
They never can Raphael it, Fuseli it, nor Blake it;   5
If they can't see an outline, pray how can they make it?
When men will draw outlines begin you to jaw them;
Madmen see outlines and therefore they draw them.

XXXII 8 Here 's two for one, what a brilliant tone *MS. 1st rdg. del.*
9, 10 A marginal addition.

XXXIV

Call that the public voice which is their error !
Like as a monkey, peeping in a mirror,
Admires all his colours brown and warm,
And never once perceives his ugly form.

ON FRIENDS AND FOES

I

I am no Homer's hero you all know ;
I profess not generosity to a foe.
My generosity is to my friends,
That for their friendship I may make amends.
The generous to enemies promotes their ends,   5
And becomes the enemy and betrayer of his friends.

II

Anger and wrath my bosom rends :
I thought them the errors of friends.
But all my limbs with warmth glow :
I find them the errors of the foe.

III

If you play a game of chance, know, before you begin,
If you are benevolent you will never win.

The Epigrams arranged in this section, all taken from the *Rossetti MS.* and
written *circa* 1807-10, refer to the unhappy period in Blake's history, when,
embittered by the treatment of Cromek, and the ungenerous attitude of con-
temporaries towards his art, culminating in Hunt's attack in the *Examiner*,
he conceived himself to be the victim of a conspiracy, and became wholly
alienated from most of his old friends. Cp. Gilchrist's *Life*, 1 (chap. 26 and
passim), Blake's *Letters*, ed. Russell, and his own references in the 'Adver-
tisement' and the *Descriptive Catalogue*.
1 6 Cp. 'Everlasting Gospel', γ 25 :

He who loves his enemies betrays his friends.

On Friends and Foes

[Of Hayley's birth]   IV

    Of H——'s birth this was the happy lot:
    His mother on his father him begot.

[On Hayley]   V

    To forgive enemies H—— does pretend,
    Who never in his life forgave a friend,
    And when he could not act upon my wife
    Hired a villain to bereave my life.

To H[ayley]   VI

    Thy friendship oft has made my heart to ache:
    Do be my enemy—for friendship's sake.

VII

On H[ayle]y's Friendship

    When H——y finds out what you cannot do,
    That is the very thing he'll set you to;
    If you break not your neck, 'tis not his fault;
    But pecks of poison are not pecks of salt.

VIII

On H[ayley] the Pickthank

    I write the rascal thanks, till he and I
    With thanks and compliments are quite drawn dry.

v 4 This line, as well as any other, may serve as an illustration of Blake's habit of embodying old-phrases, passages, or even entire stanzas in pieces written sometimes after an interval of years. Cp. with the above, composed *circa* 1809, the lines from 'Fair Elenor':

      He seeks thy love; who, coward in the night,
      Hirèd a villain to bereave my life,

probably one of the earliest poems included in the *Poetical Sketches* printed in 1783, and, according to the 'Advertisement', written at least six years earlier.

On Friends and Foes

IX

My title as a genius thus is prov'd:
Not prais'd by Hayley, nor by Flaxman lov'd.

To F[laxman] X

You call me mad, 'tis folly to do so,
To seek to turn a madman to a foe.
If you think as you speak, you are an ass;
If you do not, you are but what you was.

To F[laxman] XI

I mock thee not, though I by thee am mockèd;
Thou call'st me madman, but I call thee blockhead.

To Nancy F[laxman] XII

How can I help thy husband's copying me?
Should that make difference 'twixt me and thee?

XIII

To F[laxman] and S[tothard]

I found them blind: I taught them how to see;
And now they know neither themselves nor me.
'Tis excellent to turn a thorn to a pin,
A fool to a bolt, a knave to a glass of gin.

x 4 but what] just what *MS.* 1st rdg. del.

xiii Title] The words 'and S.' are an addition. 1 them] him *MS.* 1st rdg. del. 2 they know ... themselves] he knows ... himself *MS.* 1st rdg. del. Blake introduces this couplet into his *Descriptive Catalogue* (1809).

On Friends and Foes

To S[tothar]d   XIV

> You all your youth observ'd the golden rule,
> Till you're at last become the golden fool :
> I sport with fortune, merry, blithe and gay,
> Like to the lion sporting with his prey.
> Take you the hide and horns which you may wear,   5
> Mine is the flesh—the bones may be your share.

Cromek speaks   XV

> I always take my judgement from a fool
> Because his judgement is so very cool ;
> Not prejudiced by feelings great or small,
> Amiable state ! he cannot feel at all.

On S[tothard]   XVI

> You say reserve and modesty he has,
> Whose heart is iron, his head wood, and his face brass.
> The fox, the owl, the beetle, and the bat
> By sweet reserve and modesty get fat.

[On Stothard]   XVII

> S——, in childhood, on the nursery floor,
> Was extreme old and most extremely poor :
> He has grown old, and rich, and what he will ;
> He is extreme old, and extreme poor still.

XIV In its original form this epigram was written in the third person, 'he' for 'you', 'his' for 'your', 'he's' for 'you're' in l. 2, and 'He has' for 'Take you' in l. 5.

XV 2 Because I know he always judges cool *MS. 1st rdg. del.* 4 Amiable state !] Because we know *MS. 1st rdg. del.*

XVI 3, 4 Blake uses this couplet in his *Descriptive Catalogue*, with the change of 'owl' to 'mole' in l. 3.

On Friends and Foes

Mr. Stothard to Mr. Cromek

For Fortune's favours you your riches bring,
But Fortune says she gave you no such thing.
Why should you be ungrateful to your friends,—
Sneaking and backbiting, and odds and ends?

Mr. Cromek to Mr. Stothard

Fortune favours the brave, old proverbs say;
But not with money; that is not the way.
Turn back! turn back! you travel all in vain;
Turn through the iron gate down Sneaking Lane.

[On Cromek]   XX

Cr—— loves artists as he loves his meat:
He loves the Art; but 'tis the art to cheat.

[On Cromek]   XXI

A petty sneaking knave I knew—
O! Mr. Cr——, how do ye do?

[On P——]   XXII

P—— lovèd me not as he lov'd his friends;
For he lov'd them for gain, to serve his ends:
He lovèd me, and for no gain at all,
But to rejoice and triumph in my fall.

XXII I P——] Not, perhaps, as I formerly thought, Thomas Phillips, R.A.,
painter of the portrait of Blake engraved for Blair's *Grave*, but more probably
Sir Richard Phillips, for whom Blake executed several engravings. (See
Russell's *Engravings of William Blake*, and edition of Blake's *Letters, passim.*)
With this thumb-nail sketch of Phillips the reader may be interested to
compare the full-length portrait of 'The Publisher', drawn by George Borrow
in his *Lavengro* (Vol. II, *passim.*)

On Friends and Foes

XXIII

[On William Haines]

The Sussex men are noted fools,
And weak is their brain pan—
I wonder if H—— the painter
Is not a Sussex man.

XXIV

[On Fuseli]

The only man that e'er I knew
Who did not make me almost spew
Was Fuseli: he was both Turk and Jew—
And so, dear Christian friends, how do you do?

XXV

[To Hunt]

'Madman' I have been call'd: 'Fool' they call thee.
I wonder which they envy—thee or me?

XXVI

To H[unt]

You think Fuseli is not a great painter.   I'm glad.
This is one of the best compliments he ever had.

XXVII

[On certain Mystics]

Cosway, Frazer, and Baldwin of Egypt's lake
Fear to associate with Blake.
This life is a warfare against evils;
They heal the sick: he casts out devils.

XXIII Written about 1809, the date of the publication of Hayley's *Life of Romney*, to which William Haines and Blake both contributed engravings.

XXIV 4 dear Christian friends] sweet Christians *MS. 1st rdg. del.*

XXV, XXVI Both these epigrams, which immediately follow each other in the *MS. Book*, are evidently addressed to Hunt, and were occasioned by the reference of the latter to Fuseli and Blake in the *Examiner*, no. 75, June 4, 1809, or the later attack in no. 90, Sept. 17, 1809. Cp. also no. XXVIII, ll. 15 sqq.

214

On Friends and Foes

Hayley, Flaxman, and Stothard are also in doubt   5
Lest their virtue should be put to the rout.
One grins, t'other spits, and in corners hides,
And all the virtuous have shown their backsides.

XXVIII

—And his legs carried it like a long fork,
Reached all the way from Chichester to York,
From York all across Scotland to the sea;
This was a man of men, as seems to me.
Not only in his mouth his own soul lay,   5
But my soul also would he bear away.
Like as a pedlar bears his weary pack,
He would bear my soul buckled to his back.
But once, alas! committing a mistake,
He bore the wretched soul of William Blake   10
That he might turn it into eggs of gold;
But neither back nor mouth those eggs could hold.
His under jaw dropp'd as those eggs he laid,
And all my eggs are addled and decay'd.
The Examiner, whose very name is Hunt,   15
Call'd Death a madman, trembling for the affront

XXVIII This biographical fragment, of which the opening lines are lacking, was probably composed soon after Sept. 17, 1809, when the article on 'Mr. Blake's Exhibition' appeared in Leigh Hunt's *Examiner* (no. 90). The speaker 'Stewhard' is evidently Stothard, and the 'he' of the opening lines Cromek, elsewhere called 'Bob Screwmuch'. 'Death' is a nickname for Blake (possibly because of his association with Blair's *Grave*); 'Yorkshire Jack Hemp' for Flaxman; 'Felpham Billy' for Hayley; and 'Daddy, Jack Hemp's parson' for Dr. Malkin of the *Father's Memoirs*; while Chichester was the scene of Blake's trial for high treason at the instance of the 'Dragoon' (see Gilchrist I, chap. xix).   8, 14 I give here the original and clearer readings. Later Blake changed l. 8 to 'So Stewhard's soul he buckled to his back', and l. 14 to 'And Stewhard's eggs', &c., but failed to make corresponding changes of person in the rest of the poem.   16 trembling for the affront] Deadly the affront *MS. 1st rdg. del.*

On Friends and Foes

Like trembling hare sits on his weakly paper
On which he used to dance and sport and caper.
Yorkshire Jack Hemp and Quibble, blushing daw,
Clapp'd Death into the corner of their jaw,   20
And Felpham Billy rode out every morn,
Horseback with Death, over the fields of corn;
Who with iron hand cuff'd, in the afternoon,
The ears of Billy's Lawyer and Dragoon.
And Cur my lawyer, and Daddy, Jack Hemp's parson,   25
Both went to law with Death to keep our ears on.
For how to starve Death we had laid a plot
Against his price—but Death was in the pot.
He made them pay his price, alackaday!
He knew both Law and Gospel better than they.   30
O that I ne'er had seen that William Blake,
Or could from Death Assassinette wake!
We thought—Alas, that such a thought could be!—
That Blake would etch for him and draw for me.
For 'twas a kind of bargain Screwmuch made   35
That Blake's designs should be by us display'd,
Because he makes designs so very cheap.
Then Screwmuch at Blake's soul took a long leap.
'Twas not a mouse.   'Twas Death in a disguise.
And I, alas! live to weep out my eyes.   40
And Death sits laughing on their monuments
On which he's written ' Receivèd the contents.'
But I have writ—so sorrowful my thought is—
His epitaph; for my tears are aquafortis.
'Come, Artists, knock your head against this stone,   45
For sorrow that our friend Bob Screwmuch's gone.'
And now the Muses upon me smile and laugh
I'll also write my own dear epitaph,

19 Yorkshire] And Yorkshire *MS. 1st rdg. del.*

43, 44   But I have writ with tears, as aquafortis,
          This Epitaph—so sorrowful my thought is.   *MS. 1st rdg. del.*

On Friends and Foes

And I'll be buried near a dyke
That my friends may weep as much as they like: 50
'Here lies Stewhard the Friend of all [mankind;
He has not left one enemy behind.]'

XXIX

—For this is being a friend just in the nick,
Not when he's well, but waiting till he's sick;
He calls you to his help; be you not mov'd
Until, by being sick, his wants are prov'd.

You see him spend his soul in prophecy: 5
Do you believe it a confounded lie,
Till some bookseller, and the public fame,
Prove there is truth in his extravagant claim.

For 'tis atrocious in a friend you love
To tell you anything that he can't prove,   10
And 'tis most wicked in a Christian nation
For any man to pretend to inspiration.

XXX

Was I angry with Hayley who us'd me so ill,
Or can I be angry with Felpham's old mill?
Or angry with Flaxman, or Cromek, or Stothard,
Or poor Schiavonetti, whom they to death bother'd?
Or angry with Macklin, or Boydell, or Bowyer,   5
Because they did not say 'O what a beau ye are'?
At a friend's errors anger show,
Mirth at the errors of a foe.

51 In the MS. ' Here lies Stewhard the Friend of all, &c.'   I complete the couplet from the 'Epitaph on John Trot' (p. 221).

XXIX Following a wholly erased stanza in the *MS.*   9 atrocious⌐ most wicked *MS. 1st rdg. del.*

XXX 3 Or angry with Boydell or Bowyer or Bu[tts]] *MS. 1st rdg. del.* 5 Macklin, Boydell, Bowyer] Publishers for whom Blake engraved.   Cp. a reference to the same trio in a letter to Hayley dated 11th December, 1805 (Blake's *Letters*, ed. Russell, p. 187).

On Friends and Foes

XXXI

Having given great offence by writing in prose,
I'll write in verse as soft as Bartoloze.
Some blush at what others can see no crime in;
But nobody sees any harm in riming.
Dryden, in rime, cries 'Milton only plann'd':   5
Every fool shook his bells throughout the land.
Tom Cooke cut Hogarth down with his clean graving:
Thousands of connoisseurs with joy ran raving.
Thus, Hayley on his toilette seeing the soap,
Cries, 'Homer is very much improv'd by Pope.'   10
Some say I've given great provision to my foes,
And that now I lead my false friends by the nose.
Flaxman and Stothard, smelling a sweet savour,
Cry 'Blakified drawing spoils painter and engraver';
While I, looking up to my umbrella,   15
Resolv'd to be a very contrary fellow,
Cry, looking quite from skumference to centre:
'No one can finish so high as the original Inventor.'
Thus poor Schiavonetti died of the Cromek—
A thing that's tied around the Examiner's neck!   20
This is my sweet apology to my friends,
That I may put them in mind of their latter ends.
If men will act like a maid smiling over a churn,
They ought not, when it comes to another's turn,

XXXI 1 Cp. Hunt's reference to Blake's 'Descriptive Catalogue',
Examiner, no. 90, Sept. 17, 1809.   4 But nobody at all sees harm in
riming *MS. 1st rdg. del.*   8 How many thousands of connoisseurs
ran raving *MS. 1st rdg. del.*   9 Thus] *An addition.*   10 Cries] Says
MS. 1st rdg. del.

11, 12   I've given great provision to my foes,
      But now I'll lead my false friends by the nose. *MS. 1st rdg. del.,*
'Some say' in l. 11, and 'that' in l. 12 being marginal additions.   17 Cry
Tom Cooke proves from circumference to centre *MS. 1st rdg. del.*
19, 20 A reference to Cromek's 'Account of Mr. Schiavonetti' in the
Examiner, July 1, 1810.

To grow sour at what a friend may utter,   25
Knowing and feeling that we all have need of butter.
False friends, fie! fie! Our friendship you shan't sever;
In spite we will be greater friends than ever.

MISCELLANEOUS EPIGRAMS

I

His whole life is an epigram smart, smooth and neatly penn'd,
Plaited quite neat to catch applause, with a hang-noose at the end

II

He has observ'd the golden rule,
Till he's become the golden fool.

III

--And in melodious accents I
Will sit me down, and cry 'I! I!'

XXXI 27 fie! fie!] O no! *MS. 1st rdg. del.* you shan't] ne'er shall *MS.
1st rdg. del.* 28 In spite] For now *MS. 1st rdg. del.*

Miscellaneous Epigrams] All these (written *circa* 1807-9) are taken from
the *Rossetti MS.*, with the exception of no. XI, which is one of Blake's
marginalia in his copy of Reynolds' *Discourses*.

I 1 The first word, which is very indistinctly written, may be either 'His'
or 'Her'; all editors print the latter, but 'His' on the whole seems the
more probable reading. The same words, it may be noted, are confused in
the Song, 'Love and Harmony combine' (*Poetical Sketches*, p. 10 of this ed.).

II A variant of the first couplet of an epigram addressed to Stothard, see
p. 212, no. XIV.

III Following the prose passage in Blake's 'Advertisement' in the *MS.
Book*: 'I demand therefore of the amateurs of art the encouragement which
is my due. If they continue to refuse, theirs is the loss, not mine, and theirs
is the contempt of posterity. I have enough in the approbation of fellow
labourers. This is my glory, and my exceeding great reward. I go on, and
nothing can hinder my course.'

Miscellaneous Epigrams

IV

Some people admire the work of a fool,
For it's sure to keep your judgement cool;
It does not reproach you with want of wit;
It is not like a lawyer serving a writ.

V

He's a blockhead who wants a proof of what he can't perceive;
And he's a fool who tries to make such a blockhead believe.

VI

Great men and fools do often me inspire;
But the greater fool, the greater liar.

VII

Some men, created for destruction, come
Into the world, and make the world their home.
Be they as vile and base as e'er they can,
They'll still be callèd 'The World's Honest Man.'

An Epitaph   VIII

Come knock your heads against this stone,
For sorrow that poor John Thompson's gone.

Another   IX

I was buried near this dyke,
That my friends may weep as much as they like.

IV A variant and more general form of the epigram on Cromek, see p. 212, no. XV.

VII 3, 4   Friend Caiaphas is one, do what he can,
              He'll still be callèd 'The World's Honest Man.'
                              MS. 2nd rdg. del.

VIII, IX, X Cp. the slightly different form of these three epitaphs in the lines beginning 'And his legs carried it like a long fork', p. 215, no. XXVIII.

Miscellaneous Epigrams

Another   X

> Here lies John Trot, the friend of all mankind:
> He has not left one enemy behind.
> Friends were quite hard to find, old authors say;
> But now they stand in everybody's way.

XI

> When France got free, Europe, 'twixt fools and knaves,
> Were savage first to France, and after—slaves.

XII

On the virginity of the Virgin Mary and Johanna Southcott

> Whate'er is done to her she cannot know,
> And if you'll ask her she will swear it so.
> Whether 'tis good or evil none's to blame:
> No one can take the pride, no one the shame.

XIII

Imitation of Pope: a compliment to the Ladies

> Wondrous the gods, more wondrous are the men,
> More wondrous, wondrous still, the cock and hen,
> More wondrous still the table, stool and chair;
> But ah! more wondrous still the charming fair.

XIV

> When a man has married a wife, he finds out whether
> Her knees and elbows are only glued together.

XV

> To Chloe's breast young Cupid slyly stole,
> But he crept in at Myra's pocket-hole.

XII 2 swear it] tell you *MS. 1st rdg. del.*

TIRIEL

I

And agèd Tiriel stood before the gates of his beautiful palace
With Myratana, once the Queen of all the western plains;
But now his eyes were darkenèd, and his wife fading in death.
They stood before their once delightful palace; and thus the voice
Of agèd Tiriel arose, that his sons might hear in their gates:— 5

'Accursèd race of Tiriel! behold your father;
Come forth and look on her that bore you!   Come, you accursed
        sons!
In my weak arms I here have borne your dying mother.
Come forth, sons of the Curse, come forth! see the death of
        Myratana!'

His sons ran from their gates, and saw their agèd parents stand;
And thus the eldest son of Tiriel rais'd his mighty voice:— 11

'Old man! unworthy to be call'd the father of Tiriel's race!
For every one of those thy wrinkles, each of those grey hairs
Are cruel as death, and as obdurate as the devouring pit!
Why should thy sons care for thy curses, thou accursèd man? 15
Were we not slaves till we rebell'd?   Who cares for Tiriel's curse?
His blessing was a cruel curse; his curse may be a blessing.'

He ceas'd: the agèd man rais'd up his right hand to the heavens,
His left supported Myratana, shrinking in pangs of death:

---

1 Followed in the MS. by a del. half-line:
        But dark were his once piercing eyes . . .

The orbs of his large eyes he open'd, and thus his voice went
    forth :—   20

'Serpents, not sons, wreathing around the bones of Tiriel !
Ye worms of death, feasting upon your agèd parent's flesh !
Listen ! and hear your mother's groans !   No more accursèd sons
She bears ; she groans not at the birth of Heuxos or Yuva.
These are the groans of death, ye serpents ! these are the groans
    of death !   25
Nourish'd with milk, ye serpents, nourish'd with mother's tears
    and cares !
Look at my eyes, blind as the orbless skull among the stones !
Look at my bald head !   Hark ! listen, ye serpents, listen ! . . .
What, Myratana ! What, my wife ! O Soul ! O Spirit ! O Fire !
What, Myratana ! art thou dead ? Look here, ye serpents, look !
The serpents sprung from her own bowels have drain'd her dry
    as this.   31
Curse on your ruthless heads, for I will bury her even here !'

So saying, he began to dig a grave with his agèd hands ;
But Heuxos call'd a son of Zazel to dig their mother a grave.

' Old Cruelty, desist ! and let us dig a grave for thee.   35
Thou hast refus'd our charity, thou hast refus'd our food,
Thou hast refus'd our clothes, our beds, our houses for thy
    dwelling,
Choosing to wander like a son of Zazel in the rocks.
Why dost thou curse ?   Is not the curse now come upon your
    head ?   39
Was it not you enslav'd the sons of Zazel ?   And they have curs'd,
And now you feel it.   Dig a grave, and let us bury our mother.'

' There, take the body, cursèd sons ! and may the heavens rain wrath
As thick as northern fogs, around your gates, to choke you up !
That you may lie as now your mother lies, like dogs cast out,
The stink of your dead carcases annoying man and beast,   45
Till your white bones are bleach'd with age for a memorial.

No! your remembrance shall perish; for, when your carcases
Lie stinking on the earth, the buriers shall arise from the East,
And not a bone of all the sons of Tiriel remain.
Bury your mother! but you cannot bury the curse of Tiriel.'   50

He ceas'd, and darkling o'er the mountains sought his pathless
way.

II

He wander'd day and night: to him both day and night were
dark.
The sun he felt, but the bright moon was now a useless globe:
O'er mountains and thro' vales of woe the blind and agèd man
Wander'd, till he that leadeth all led him to the vales of Har.   55

And Har and Heva, like two children, sat beneath the oak:
Mnetha, now agèd, waited on them, and brought them food and
clothing;
But they were as the shadow of Har, and as the years forgotten.
Playing with flowers and running after birds they spent the day,
And in the night like infants slept, delighted with infant dreams.

Soon as the blind wanderer enter'd the pleasant gardens of Har,
They ran weeping, like frighted infants, for refuge in Mnetha's
arms.   62
The blind man felt his way, and cried: 'Peace to these open
doors!
Let no one fear, for poor blind Tiriel hurts none but himself.
Tell me, O friends, where am I now, and in what pleasant place?'

'This is the valley of Har,' said Mnetha, 'and this the tent of
Har.   66
Who art thou, poor blind man, that takest the name of Tiriel on
thee?
Tiriel is King of all the West. Who art thou? I am Mnetha;
And this is Har and Heva, trembling like infants by my side.'

Tiriel

'I know Tiriel is King of the West, and there he lives in joy. 70
No matter who I am, O Mnetha! If thou hast any food,
Give it me; for I cannot stay; my journey is far from hence.'

Then Har said: 'O my mother Mnetha, venture not so near him;
For he is the king of rotten wood, and of the bones of death; 74
He wanders without eyes, and passes thro' thick walls and doors.
Thou shalt not smite my mother Mnetha, O thou eyeless man!'

'A wanderer, I beg for food: you see I cannot weep:
I cast away my staff, the kind companion of my travel,
And I kneel down that you may see I am a harmless man.'

He kneelèd down. And Mnetha said: 'Come, Har and Heva,
    rise! 80
He is an innocent old man, and hungry with his travel.'

Then Har arose, and laid his hand upon old Tiriel's head.

'God bless thy poor bald pate! God bless thy hollow winking
    eyes!
God bless thy shrivell'd beard! God bless thy many-wrinkled
    forehead!
Thou hast no teeth, old man! and thus I kiss thy sleek bald
    head. 85
Heva, come kiss his bald head, for he will not hurt us, Heva.

Then Heva came, and took old Tiriel in her mother's arms.

'Bless thy poor eyes, old man, and bless the old father of Tiriel!
Thou art my Tiriel's old father; I know thee thro' thy wrinkles,
Because thou smellest like the fig-tree, thou smellest like ripe
    figs.

76 Followed by a del. line :

    O venerable, O most piteous, O most woeful day!

78 Followed by a del. line :

    But I can kneel down at your door. I am a harmless man.

Tiriel

How didst thou lose thy eyes, old Tiriel? Bless thy wrinkled
    face!'   91

Mnetha said: 'Come in, agèd wanderer! tell us of thy name.
Why shouldest thou conceal thyself from those of thine own
    flesh?'

'I am not of this region,' said Tiriel dissemblingly.
'I am an agèd wanderer, once father of a race   95
Far in the North; but they were wicked, and were all destroy'd,
And I their father sent an outcast. I have told you all.
Ask me no more, I pray, for grief hath seal'd my precious sight.'

'O Lord!' said Mnetha, 'how I tremble! Are there then more
    people,
More human creatures on this earth, beside the sons of Har?'

'No more,' said Tiriel, 'but I, remain on all this globe;   101
And I remain an outcast. Hast thou anything to drink?

Then Mnetha gave him milk and fruits, and they sat down
    together.

III

They sat and ate, and Har and Heva smil'd on Tiriel.

'Thou art a very old old man, but I am older than thou.   105
How came thine hair to leave thy forehead? how came thy face so
    brown?
My hair is very long, my beard doth cover all my breast.

---

91 Followed by two del. lines:
    The agèd Tiriel could not speak, his heart was full of grief;
    He strove against his rising passions, but still he could not speak.
94 Followed by a del. line:
    Fearing to tell them who he was, because of the weakness of Har.

God bless thy piteous face! To count the wrinkles in thy face
Would puzzle Mnetha. Bless thy face! for thou art Tiriel.'

'Tiriel I never saw but once: I sat with him and ate;   110
He was as cheerful as a prince, and gave me entertainment;
But long I stay'd not at his palace, for I am forc'd to wander.'

'What! wilt thou leave us too?' said Heva: 'thou shalt not leave
   us too,
For we have many sports to show thee, and many songs to sing;
And after dinner we will walk into the cage of Har,   115
And thou shalt help us to catch birds, and gather them ripe
   cherries.
Then let thy name be Tiriel, and never leave us more.'

'If thou dost go,' said Har, 'I wish thine eyes may see thy folly.
My sons have left me; did thine leave thee? O, 'twas very cruel!'

'No! venerable man,' said Tiriel, 'ask me not such things,   120
For thou dost make my heart to bleed: my sons were not like thine,
But worse. O never ask me more, or I must flee away!

'Thou shalt not go,' said Heva, 'till thou hast seen our singing-
   birds,
And heard Har sing in the great cage, and slept upon our fleeces.
Go not! for thou art so like Tiriel that I love thine head,   125
Tho' it is wrinkled like the earth parch'd with the summer heat.'

Then Tiriel rose up from the seat, and said: 'God bless these tents!
My journey is o'er rocks and mountains, not in pleasant vales:
I must not sleep nor rest, because of madness and dismay.'

109 Followed by two del. lines:
    Tiriel could scarce·dissemble more, and his tongue could scarce refrain,
    But still he fear'd that Har and Heva would die of joy and grief.
127 Followed by a del. line:
        God bless my benefactors, for I cannot tarry longer.
129 Followed by a del. line:
    Then Mnetha led him to the door and gave to him his staff.

And Mnetha said: 'Thou must not go to wander dark, alone; 130
But dwell with us, and let us be to thee instead of eyes,
And I will bring thee food, old man, till death shall call thee hence.

Then Tiriel frown'd, and answer'd: 'Did I not command you,
    saying,
"Madness and deep dismay possess the heart of the blind man,
The wanderer who seeks the woods, leaning upon his staff?"' 135

Then Mnetha, trembling at his frowns, led him to the tent door,
And gave to him his staff, and bless'd him.   He went on his way.

But Har and Heva stood and watch'd him till he enter'd the wood;
And then they went and wept to Mnetha: but they soon forgot
    their tears.

IV

Over the weary hills the blind man took his lonely way;   140
To him the day and night alike was dark and desolate;

But far he had not gone when Ijim from his woods came down,
Met him at entrance of the forest, in a dark and lonely way.

'Who art thou, eyeless wretch, that thus obstruct'st the lion's
    path?
Ijim shall rend thy feeble joints, thou tempter of dark Ijim! 145
Thou hast the form of Tiriel, but I know thee well enough.
Stand from my path, foul fiend!   Is this the last of thy deceits,
To be a hypocrite, and stand in shape of a blind beggar?'

The blind man heard his brother's voice, and kneel'd down on
    his knee.

'O brother Ijim, if it is thy voice that speaks to me,   150
Smite not thy brother Tiriel, tho' weary of his life.
My sons have smitten me already; and, if thou smitest me,
The curse that rolls over their heads will rest itself on thine.
'Tis now seven years since in my palace I beheld thy face.'

154 Followed by a del. line:
        Seven years of sorrow; then the curse of Zazel . . .

Tiriel

Come, thou dark fiend, I dare thy cunning! know that Ijim 155
    scorns
To smite thee in the form of helpless age and eyeless policy.
Rise up! for I discern thee, and I dare thy eloquent tongue.
Come! I will lead thee on thy way, and use thee as a scoff.'

'O brother Ijim, thou beholdest wretched Tiriel:
Kiss me, my brother, and then leave me to wander desolate!' 160

'No! artful fiend, but I will lead thee; dost thou want to go?
Reply not, lest I bind thee with the green flags of the brook.
Aye! now thou art discover'd, I will use thee like a slave.'

When Tiriel heard the words of Ijim, he sought not to reply:
He knew 'twas vain, for Ijim's words were as the voice of Fate.

And they went on together, over hills, thro' woody dales, 166
Blind to the pleasures of the sight, and deaf to warbling birds:
All day they walk'd, and all the night beneath the pleasant moon,
Westwardly journeying, till Tiriel grew weary with his travel.

'O Ijim, I am faint and weary, for my knees forbid 170
To bear me further: urge me not, lest I should die with travel.
A little rest I crave, a little water from a brook,
Or I shall soon discover that I am a mortal man,
And you will lose your once-lov'd Tiriel. Alas! how faint I am!'

'Impudent fiend!' said Ijim, 'hold thy glib and eloquent tongue!
Tiriel is a king, and thou the tempter of dark Ijim. 176
Drink of this running brook, and I will bear thee on my shoulders.'

He drank; and Ijim rais'd him up, and bore him on his shoulders:
All day he bore him; and, when evening drew her solemn curtain,
Enter'd the gates of Tiriel's palace, and stood and call'd aloud:—

'Heuxos, come forth! I here have brought the fiend that troubles
    Ijim. 181
Look! know'st thou aught of this grey beard, or of these blinded
    eyes?'

Heuxos and Lotho ran forth at the sound of Ijim's voice,
And saw their agèd father borne upon his mighty shoulders.
Their eloquent tongues were dumb, and sweat stood on their
    trembling limbs :   185
They knew 'twas vain to strive with Ijim.   They bow'd and silent
    stood.

'What, Heuxos ! call thy father, for I mean to sport to-night.
This is the hypocrite that sometimes roars a dreadful lion ;
Then I have rent his limbs, and left him rotting in the forest
For birds to eat. But I have scarce departed from the place, 190
But like a tiger he would come : and so I rent him too.
Then like a river he would seek to drown me in his waves ;
But soon I buffeted the torrent : anon like to a cloud
Fraught with the swords of lightning ; but I brav'd the vengeance
    too.
Then he would creep like a bright serpent ; till around my neck,
While I was sleeping, he would twine : I squeez'd his poisonous
    soul.   196
Then like a toad, or like a newt, would whisper in my ears ;
Or like a rock stood in my way, or like a poisonous shrub.
At last I caught him in the form of Tiriel, blind and old,   199
And so I'll keep him ! Fetch your father, fetch forth Myratana !'

They stood confounded, and thus Tiriel rais'd his silver voice :—

'Serpents, not sons, why do you stand ? Fetch hither Tiriel !
Fetch hither Myratana ! and delight yourselves with scoffs ;
For poor blind Tiriel is return'd, and this much-injur'd head
Is ready for your bitter taunts. Come forth, sons of the
    Curse !'

Meantime the other sons of Tiriel ran around their father,   206
Confounded at the terrible strength of Ijim : they knew 'twas
    vain.
Both spear and shield were useless, and the coat of iron mail,

When Ijim stretch'd his mighty arm; the arrow from his limbs
Rebounded, and the piercing sword broke on his naked flesh. 210

'Then is it true, Heuxos, that thou hast turn'd thy agèd parent
To be the sport of wintry winds?' said Ijim, 'is this true?
It is a lie, and I am like the tree torn by the wind,
Thou eyeless fiend, and you dissemblers! Is this Tiriel's house?
It is as false as Matha, and as dark as vacant Orcus.   215
Escape, ye fiends! for Ijim will not lift his hand against ye.'

So saying, Ijim gloomy turn'd his back, and silent sought
The secret forests, and all night wander'd in desolate ways.

v

And agèd Tiriel stood and said: 'Where does the thunder sleep?
Where doth he hide his terrible head? And his swift and fiery
        daughters,   220
Where do they shroud their fiery wings, and the terrors of their
        hair?
Earth, thus I stamp thy bosom! Rouse the earthquake from his
        den,
To raise his dark and burning visage thro' the cleaving ground,
To thrust these towers with his shoulders! Let his fiery dogs
Rise from the centre, belching flames and roarings, dark smoke! 225
Where art thou, Pestilence, that bathest in fogs and standing lakes?

210 Followed by the del. lines:

> Then Ijim said: 'Lotho, Clithyma, Makuth, fetch your father!
> Why do you stand confounded thus? Heuxos, why art thou silent?'
>
> 'O noble Ijim, thou hast brought our father to our eyes,
> That we may tremble and repent before thy mighty knees.
> O! we are but the slaves of Fortune, and that most cruel man
> Desires our deaths, O Ijim! . . .
>   . . . if the eloquent voice of Tiriel
> Hath work'd our ruin, we submit nor strive against stern fate.'
>
> He spoke, kneel'd upon his knee. Then Ijim on the pavement
> Set agèd Tiriel in deep thought whether these things were so.

Rise up thy sluggish limbs, and let the loathsomest of poisons
Drop from thy garments as thou walkest, wrapp'd in yellow clouds!
Here take thy seat in this wide court; let it be strewn with dead;
And sit and smile upon these cursèd sons of Tiriel!   230
Thunder, and fire, and pestilence, hear you not Tiriel's curse?'
He ceas'd. The heavy clouds confus'd roll'd round the lofty
    towers,
Discharging their enormous voices at the father's curse.
The earth tremblèd; fires belchèd from the yawning clefts;
And when the shaking ceas'd, a fog possess'd the accursèd clime.

The cry was great in Tiriel's palace: his five daughters ran,   236
And caught him by the garments, weeping with cries of bitter woe.

'Aye, now you feel the curse, you cry! but may all ears be deaf
As Tiriel's, and all eyes as blind as Tiriel's to your woes!
May never stars shine on your roofs! may never sun nor moon   240
Visit you, but eternal fogs hover around your walls!
Hela, my youngest daughter, you shall lead me from this place;
And let the curse fall on the rest, and wrap them up together!'

He ceas'd: and Hela led her father from the noisome place.
In haste they fled; while all the sons and daughters of Tiriel,   245
Chain'd in thick darkness, utterèd cries of mourning all the night.
And in the morning, lo! an hundred men in ghastly death!
The four daughters, stretch'd on the marble pavement, silent all,
Fall'n by the pestilence!—the rest mop'd round in guilty fears;
And all the children in their beds were cut off in one night.   250
Thirty of Tiriel's sons remain'd, to wither in the palace,
Desolate, loathèd, dumb, astonish'd—waiting for black death.

VI

And Hela led her father thro' the silence of the night,
Astonish'd, silent, till the morning beams began to spring.

'Now, Hela, I can go with pleasure, and dwell with Har and Heva,
Now that the curse shall clean devour all those guilty sons.   256

This is the right and ready way; I know it by the sound

That our feet make. Remember, Hela, I have savèd thee from death;

Then be obedient to thy father, for the curse is taken off thee.

I dwelt with Myratana five years in the desolate rock;   260

And all that time we waited for the fire to fall from heaven,

Or for the torrents of the sea to overwhelm you all.

But now my wife is dead, and all the time of grace is past:

You see the parent's curse. Now lead me where I have commanded.'

'O leaguèd with evil spirits, thou accursèd man of sin!   265

True, I was born thy slave! Who ask'd thee to save me from death?

'Twas for thyself, thou cruel man, because thou wantest eyes.'

'True, Hela, this is the desert of all those cruel ones.

Is Tiriel cruel? Look! his daughter, and his youngest daughter,

Laughs at affection, glories in rebellion, scoffs at love.   270

I have not ate these two days. Lead me to Har and Heva's tent,

Or I will wrap thee up in such a terrible father's curse

That thou shalt feel worms in thy marrow creeping thro' thy bones.

Yet thou shalt lead me! Lead me, I command, to Har and Heva!'

'O cruel! O destroyer! O consumer! O avenger!   275

To Har and Heva I will lead thee: then would that they would curse!

Then would they curse as thou hast cursèd! But they are not like thee!

O! they are holy and forgiving, fill'd with loving mercy,

Forgetting the offences of their most rebellious children,

Or else thou wouldest not have liv'd to curse thy helpless children.'

'Look on my eyes, Hela, and see, for thou hast eyes to see.   281

The tears swell from my stony fountains. Wherefore do I weep?

Wherefore from my blind orbs art thou not seiz'd with poisonous
    stings?
Laugh, serpent, youngest venomous reptile of the flesh of Tiriel!
Laugh! for thy father Tiriel shall give thee cause to laugh,   285
Unless thou lead me to the tent of Har, child of the Curse!'

'Silence thy evil tongue, thou murderer of thy helpless children!
I lead thee to the tent of Har; not that I mind thy curse,
But that I feel they will curse thee, and hang upon thy bones
Fell shaking agonies, and in each wrinkle of that face   290
Plant worms of death to feast upon the tongue of terrible curses.'

'Hela, my daughter, listen! thou art the daughter of Tiriel.
Thy father calls. Thy father lifts his hand unto the heavens,
For thou hast laughèd at my tears, and curs'd thy agèd father.
Let snakes rise from thy bedded locks, and laugh among thy
    curls!'   295

He ceas'd. Her dark hair upright stood, while snakes
    infolded round
Her madding brows: her shrieks appall'd the soul of Tiriel.

'What have I done, Hela, my daughter? Fear'st thou now the
    curse,
Or wherefore dost thou cry? Ah, wretch, to curse thy agèd
    father!
Lead me to Har and Heva, and the curse of Tiriel   300
Shall fail. If thou refuse, howl in the desolate mountains!'

VII

She, howling, led him over mountains and thro' frighted vales,
Till to the caves of Zazel they approach'd at eventide.
Forth from their caves old Zazel and his sons ran, when they saw
Their tyrant prince blind, and his daughter howling and leading
    him.   305

They laugh'd and mockèd; some threw dirt and stones as they
    pass'd by;
But when Tiriel turn'd around and rais'd his awful voice,
Some fled away; but Zazel stood still, and thus begun:—

'Bald tyrant, wrinkled cunning, listen to Zazel's chains!
'Twas thou that chainèd thy brother Zazel! Where are now
    thine eyes?   310
Shout, beautiful daughter of Tiriel! thou singest a sweet song!
Where are you going? Come and eat some roots, and drink
    some water.
Thy crown is bald, old man; the sun will dry thy brains away,
And thou wilt be as foolish as thy foolish brother Zazel.'

The blind man heard, and smote his breast, and trembling
    passèd on.   315
They threw dirt after them, till to the covert of a wood
The howling maiden led her father, where wild beasts resort,
Hoping to end her woes; but from her cries the tigers fled.
All night they wander'd thro' the wood; and when the sun
    arose,
They enter'd on the mountains of Har: at noon the happy tents
Were frighted by the dismal cries of Hela on the mountains.   321

But Har and Heva slept fearless as babes on loving breasts.
Mnetha awoke: she ran and stood at the tent door, and saw
The agèd wanderer led towards the tents; she took her bow,
And chose her arrows, then advanc'd to meet the terrible pair.   325

VIII

And Mnetha hasted, and met them at the gate of the lower
    garden.
'Stand still or from my bow receive a sharp and wingèd death!'

Then Tiriel stood, saying: 'What soft voice threatens such bitter
    things?
Lead me to Har and Heva; I am Tiriel, King of the West.'

And Mnetha led them to the tent of Har; and Har and Heva
Ran to the door. When Tiriel felt the ankles of agèd Har,   331
He said: 'O weak mistaken father of a lawless race,
Thy laws, O Har, and Tiriel's wisdom, end together in a curse.

Why is one law given to the lion and the patient ox?
And why men bound beneath the heavens in a reptile form,   335
A worm of sixty winters creeping on the dusky ground?
The child springs from the womb; the father ready stands to form
The infant head, while the mother idle plays with her dog on her
    couch:
The young bosom is cold for lack of mother's nourishment, and milk
Is cut off from the weeping mouth with difficulty and pain: 340
The little lids are lifted, and the little nostrils open'd:
The father forms a whip to rouse the sluggish senses to act,
And scourges off all youthful fancies from the new-born man.
Then walks the weak infant in sorrow, compell'd to number
    footsteps
Upon the sand. And when the drone has reach'd his crawling
    length,   345

    333 Followed by a del. half-line:
            Thy God of Love, thy Heaven of Joy . . .
    334 Followed by the del. lines:
Dost thou not see that men cannot be formèd all alike,
Some nostril'd wide, breathing out blood; some close shut up
In silent deceit, poisons inhaling from the morning rose,
With daggers hid beneath their lips and poison in their tongue;
Or eyed with little sparks of Hell, or with infernal brands,
Flinging flames of discontent and plagues of dark despair;
Or those whose mouths are graves, whose teeth the gates of eternal death.
Can wisdom be put in a silver rod, or love in a golden bowl?
Is the sun a king, warmed without wool? or does he cry with a voice
Of thunder? Does he look upon the sun, and laugh or stretch
His little hands unto the depths of the sea, to bring forth
The deadly cunning of the scaly tribe, and spread it to the morning?

Tiriel

Black berries appear that poison all round him.   Such was Tiriel,
Compell'd to pray repugnant, and to humble the immortal spirit ;
Till I am subtil as a serpent in a paradise,
Consuming all, both flowers and fruits, insects and warbling birds.
And now my paradise is fall'n, and a drear sandy plain   350
Returns my thirsty hissings in a curse on thee, O Har,
Mistaken father of a lawless race !—My voice is past.'

He ceas'd, outstretch'd at Har and Heva's feet in awful death.

346 Followed by a del. line :
      Hypocrisy, the idiot's wisdom, and the wise man's folly.

THE

BOOK OF THEL

(Engraved 1789)

Thel's Motto.

> Does the Eagle know what is in the pit
> Or wilt thou go ask the Mole?
> Can Wisdom be put in a silver rod,
> Or Love in a golden bowl?

I

The daughters of [the] Seraphim led round their sunny flocks— 5
All but the youngest: she in paleness sought the secret air,
To fade away like morning beauty from her mortal day:
Down by the river of Adona her soft voice is heard,
And thus her gentle lamentation falls like morning dew:—

'O life of this our spring! why fades the lotus of the water? 10
Why fade these children of the spring, born but to smile and fall?
Ah! Thel is like a wat'ry bow, and like a parting cloud;
Like a reflection in a glass; like shadows in the water;
Like dreams of infants, like a smile upon an infant's face;
Like the dove's voice; like transient day; like music in the air. 15
Ah! gentle may I lay me down, and gentle rest my head,
And gentle sleep the sleep of death, and gentle hear the voice
Of Him that walketh in the garden in the evening time.'

The Lily of the Valley, breathing in the humble grass,
Answerèd the lovely maid and said: 'I am a wat'ry weed, 20
And I am very small, and love to dwell in lowly vales;

The Book of Thel

So weak, the gilded butterfly scarce perches on my head.
Yet I am visited from heaven, and He that smiles on all
Walks in the valley, and each morn over me spreads His hand,
Saying, " Rejoice, thou humble grass, thou new-born lily-flower, 25
Thou gentle maid of silent valleys and of modest brooks ;
For thou shalt be clothèd in light, and fed with morning manna,
Till summer's heat melts thee beside the fountains and the springs,
To flourish in eternal vales."   Then why should Thel complain ?
Why should the mistress of the vales of Har utter a sigh ?' 30

She ceas'd, and smil'd in tears, then sat down in her silver shrine.

Thel answer'd : ' O thou little Virgin of the peaceful valley,
Giving to those that cannot crave, the voiceless, the o'ertired ;
Thy breath doth nourish the innocent lamb, he smells thy milky
garments,
He crops thy flowers while thou sittest smiling in his face, 35
Wiping his mild and meeking mouth from all contagious taints.
Thy wine doth purify the golden honey ; thy perfume,
Which thou dost scatter on every little blade of grass that springs,
Revives the milkèd cow, and tames the fire-breathing steed.
But Thel is like a faint cloud kindled at the rising sun : 40
I vanish from my pearly throne, and who shall find my place ?'

' Queen of the vales,' the Lily answer'd, ' ask the tender Cloud,
And it shall tell thee why it glitters in the morning sky,
And why it scatters its bright beauty thro' the humid air.
Descend, O little Cloud, and hover before the eyes of Thel.' 45

The Cloud descended, and the Lily bowèd her modest head,
And went to mind her numerous charge among the verdant grass.

II

' O little Cloud,' the Virgin said, ' I charge thee tell to me
Why thou complainest not, when in one hour thou fade away :
Then we shall seek thee, but not find.   Ah ! Thel is like to thee :
I pass away : yet I complain, and no one hears my voice.' 51

The Book of Thel

The Cloud then show'd his golden head and his bright form
    emerg'd,
Hovering and glittering on the air before the face of Thei.

'O Virgin, know'st thou not our steeds drink of the golden springs
Where Luvah doth renew his horses? Look'st thou on my youth, 55
And fearest thou, because I vanish and am seen no more,
Nothing remains?   O Maid, I tell thee, when I pass away,
It is to tenfold life, to love, to peace, and raptures holy:
Unseen descending, weigh my light wings upon balmy flowers,
And court the fair-eyed dew, to take me to her shining tent: 60
The weeping virgin, trembling, kneels before the risen sun,
Till we arise link'd in a golden band and never part,
But walk united, bearing food to all our tender flowers.'

'Dost thou, O little Cloud?   I fear that I am not like thee,
For I walk thro' the vales of Har, and smell the sweetest flowers,
But I feed not the little flowers; I hear the warbling birds,   66
But I feed not the warbling birds; they fly and seek their food:
But Thel delights in these no more, because I fade away;
And all shall say, "Without a use this shining woman liv'd,
Or did she only live to be at death the food of worms?"'   70

The Cloud reclin'd upon his airy throne, and answer'd thus :—

'Then if thou art the food of worms, O Virgin of the skies,
How great thy use, how great thy blessing!   Everything that lives
Lives not alone nor for itself.   Fear not, and I will call
The weak Worm from its lowly bed, and thou shalt hear its voice.
Come forth, Worm of the silent valley, to thy pensive Queen.' 76

The helpless Worm arose, and sat upon the Lily's leaf,
And the bright Cloud sail'd on, to find his partner in the vale.

III

Then Thel astonish'd view'd the Worm upon its dewy bed.

'Art thou a Worm?   Image of weakness, art thou but a Worm?
I see thee like an infant wrappèd in the Lily's leaf.   81

Ah! weep not, little voice, thou canst not speak, but thou canst
    weep.
Is this a Worm?   I see thee lay helpless and naked, weeping,
And none to answer, none to cherish thee with mother's smiles.'

The Clod of Clay heard the Worm's voice and rais'd her pitying
    head: 85
She bow'd over the weeping infant, and her life exhal'd
In milky fondness: then on Thel she fix'd her humble eyes.

'O Beauty of the vales of Har! we live not for ourselves.
Thou seest me, the meanest thing, and so I am indeed.
My bosom of itself is cold, and of itself is dark;   90
But He, that loves the lowly, pours His oil upon my head,
And kisses me, and binds His nuptial bands around my breast,
And says: "Thou mother of my children, I have lovèd thee,
And I have given thee a crown that none can take away."
But how this is, sweet Maid, I know not, and I cannot know; 95
I ponder, and I cannot ponder; yet I live and love.'

The Daughter of Beauty wip'd her pitying tears with her white
    veil,
And said: 'Alas! I knew not this, and therefore did I weep.
That God would love a worm I knew, and punish the evil foot
That wilful bruis'd its helpless form; but that He cherish'd it 100
With milk and oil I never knew, and therefore did I weep;
And I complain'd in the mild air, because I fade away,
And lay me down in thy cold bed, and leave my shining lot.'

'Queen of the vales,' the matron Clay answer'd, 'I heard thy sighs,
And all thy moans flew o'er my roof, but I have call'd them down.
Wilt thou, O Queen, enter my house? 'Tis given thee to enter 106
And to return: fear nothing, enter with thy virgin feet.'

IV

The eternal gates' terrific Porter lifted the northern bar:
Thel enter'd in and saw the secrets of the land unknown.
She saw the couches of the dead, and where the fibrous roots 110

Of every heart on earth infixes deep its restless twists:
A land of sorrows and of tears where never smile was seen.

She wander'd in the land of clouds thro' valleys dark, list'ning
Dolours and lamentations; waiting oft beside a dewy grave
She stood in silence, list'ning to the voices of the ground,   115
Till to her own grave-plot she came, and there she sat down,
And heard this voice of sorrow breathèd from the hollow pit.

'Why cannot the Ear be closèd to its own destruction?
Or the glist'ning Eye to the poison of a smile?
Why are Eyelids stor'd with arrows ready drawn,   120
Where a thousand fighting men in ambush lie,
Or an Eye of gifts and graces show'ring fruits and coinèd gold?
Why a Tongue impress'd with honey from every wind?
Why an Ear, a whirlpool fierce to draw creations in?
Why a Nostril wide inhaling terror, trembling, and affright?   125
Why a tender curb upon the youthful, burning boy?
Why a little curtain of flesh on the bed of our desire?'

The Virgin started from her seat, and with a shriek
Fled back unhinder'd till she came into the vales of Har.

THE END.

PENGUIN POPULAR POETRY